Warman's
COMPANION

DEPRESSION

GLASS

Ellen T. Schroy

©2007 Krause Publications

Published by

krause publications
An Imprint of F+W Publications

700 East State Street • Iola, WI 54990-0001
715-445-2214 • 888-457-2873
www.krausebooks.com

Our toll-free number to place an order or obtain
a free catalog is (800) 258-0929.

Library of Congress Catalog Number: 2006930829

ISBN 13-digit: 978-0-89689-464-8

Designed by David Jensen and Marilyn McGrane
Edited by Dan Brownell

Printed in China

Contents

Patterns

Introduction

Welcome to *Depression Glass Warman's® Companion*. This book is designed to give collectors a basic overview of Depression-era glassware. Each pattern is represented by one or more color photographs and a line drawing to help with the identification process, along with a listing of known manufactured items and current prices to help establish the value. The pattern name listed is the one given by the manufacturer, except in the case of numbered patterns, which have now developed more easily recognizable names. Also included is a quick identification guide that sorts glassware by motif, such as circles, fruits, florals, etc.

Moderntone, cobalt blue dinner plate, **$20**; salad plate, **$12.50**; sherbet (on pedestal), **$15**; cream soup, **$25**; cup, **$18**, and saucer, **$5**.

What Is Depression Glass?

There are two categories of glassware that really have the wrong names: Depression glass and carnival class. Why and how did this happen? The names we use today were coined by folks in the late 1940s and early 1950s when collecting antiques was coming into vogue. It was when the automobile allowed people to travel freely about and enjoy Sunday rides into the country that collecting antiques became popular. Almost every little town had a dusty shop or two filled with old things, and the sign out front simply read, "Antiques." If it was old, belonged to someone's great aunt, or had lived out its usefulness, it was described as an antique. Most Americans lived in places where, when one generation died off, their belongings were usually dispersed among the younger generation or sold at house auctions. These kinds of venues allowed the young people to pay a few pennies for useful household goods that they hopefully could use for a few more years. As the country grew and the machine age became part of everyday life, some began to realize that the early culture and tools of our ancestors were becoming lost, so efforts were made to save these things, either in a museum setting, or by private investors who gathered them up.

As our culture started to embrace using old items as decorative accessories, dealers and shops began to spring up. By the early 1950s, entrepreneurs such as E. G. Warman realized that this vastly unregulated hobby was growing and perhaps publishing a price guide would help this new breed of collector realize that those old things they had in their cupboards, stashed in the barn, etc. had some value. However, to be able to organize things, you've got to name them.

By this time, people had begun to call old antique pressed glass "pattern glass" because of the hundreds of patterns associated with it, and also because a new name for the pretty colored glassware had to be developed. Because many people associated this pretty colored glassware as being made later than early American pattern glass, they began to call it "Depression glass," as that was the economic period that had most affected their lives. Today's Depression glass collectors embrace colored glassware that was made from the early 1920s up to the 1970s, as Depression glass stretched that period much longer than the name implies. Carnival glass was made from 1905 up to the early 1930s as the affordable answer to expensive art glass for the average consumer, but because much of it was sold as remainders to carnival vendors, the name "carnival glass" stuck.

Yorktown, yellow sandwich server with gold metal center handle, **$4.50**.

Much of what we know today about Depression glass is thanks to a dedicated researcher, Hazel Marie Weatherman. Mrs. Weatherman noticed that no one really knew the origins of the pretty colored glass she nicknamed "candy glass." She also knew that many of the manufacturers of this pretty glassware were going out of business and some had already disappeared. By the early 1970s, Weatherman decided someone had to document these glassmakers and their wares, so she wrote *Colored Glassware of the Depression Era*, which has become a Holy Grail for Depression glass collectors. She actually had enough material for two books, but it is her first book that remains a standard reference today.

Weatherman was a fierce researcher and she personally went to the areas where the factories were located. She spent time with the owners and the designers, documenting their recollections and copying factory catalogs. Weatherman was known to go door-to-door trying to find workers who had created her pretty candy glass.

As she recorded their stories, she learned much about the rich history of the glassmaking industry that was centered in western Pennsylvania, West Virginia, and Ohio. Weatherman and her assistant spent long hours in libraries scouring through newspapers, trade journals, and company materials. As with many types of oral histories, sometimes contradictions surfaced, but Weatherman wouldn't give up until she got to the root of the history. She used original company documents as often as possible.

By the time she was finished, she had uncovered and written about more than 40 glassmakers, where they were located, what they made, what colors they used, and everything else she could find out. Weatherman's research revealed that the peak period of production for this pretty "candy glass" was between the 1920s and the late 1930s, and "Depression glass" became part of the collecting vocabulary. From the time the term was coined, it became popular with collectors, who used it rather than specific company names such as Jeannette Glass or Hocking Glass. By collecting "Depression glass," they opened the door to hundreds of patterns, shapes, and colors.

What Weatherman discovered was that as the pattern glass industry was winding down, American glassware manufacturers were starting to look ahead to create new glassware they hoped would end up on everyone's table.

Royal Ruby, footed sugar, **$8**; footed creamer (on pedestal), **$10**; square cup, **$7.50**; square saucer, **$4**.

The manufacturers thought that through industrialization of the glassware craft, they could provide more products less expensively.

By the beginning of the 1900s, innovations were starting to come onto the scene that would allow mass-produced glass in more brilliant colors than ever before. American consumers trusted glassware to be sturdy, sanitary, and a big part of their everyday lives. When manufacturers began to experiment with color, intricate impressed patterns, and more forms than ever before, the American consumer was delighted. By the early 1920s, the heavy financial investment made by the glass manufacturers looked like it might work, until the stock market crashed and the world seemed to come to a screeching halt. When the resulting economic depression caused the manufacturers to cut back in their design department and forced them to make their ingredients go further, their colors became washed out and pale. They made the pressed glass as thin as possible so it could be made quicker and cheaper. Many manufacturers found themselves so strapped financially they were forced to declare bankruptcy. When that happened, it wasn't unusual to find another company buying molds and equipment, and luring trained employees to their factories.

Another thing that was changing in the glassware marketplace was how the word was getting out about what patterns, colors, and forms were being introduced by each company. For years before the Depression and even afterward, it was common for glass companies to send their brightest sales people to a trade show held annually in Pittsburgh. The trade journals of the time ran articles about who was there, what was new in their lines, who the top salesmen were, and who was buying. Here they eagerly waited with their order blanks for the buyers from merchandisers such as Wanamakers to come and see what was new. The new mass-marketers, like F. W. Woolworth, also came and began to order glassware.

The companies were fiercely competitive and ideas for patterns and colors were often copied and imitated. One example of this is the Cube pattern, made by Jeannette Glass Company from 1929 to 1933. Jeannette made this pattern in several colors, but it was Fostoria's American pattern that caught on with many more collectors. Fostoria created this pattern in 1915 and continued it until 1986. Its production was mostly in a brilliant crystal, but Fostoria certainly created more forms and shapes than ever found in Cube pattern. Fostoria took its production up a notch, too, when it began to advertise in the new ladies magazines of the day. For the first time, women could use their leisure time to browse through magazines that taught them how to cook, dress, and keep house. On those same pages were advertisements luring them to buy Fostoria's American pattern as well as the company's other beautiful patterns. The Fenton Glass Company also soon mastered the new world of print ads, and these two giant American glassmakers were able to last long after the economic depression had wrought such havoc on the industry.

Savvy marketing was combined with new colors and designs and more forms than ever before, so it is easy to understand why American consumers were eager to embrace this pretty new glassware and buy bridge sets, liquor sets, and all kinds of tableware. These new patterns were made to use from breakfast until bedtime, and manufacturers were as eager to sell as consumers were to buy, until the bottom fell out of the stock market and the average consumer's buying power plummeted. However, again clever marketing stepped in and events such as "dish night" at local movie theaters became a way for glass lovers to add new pieces to their sets. Soap manufacturers packed tumblers and all sorts of glassware pieces as giveaways in their boxes. Eventually, though, the bubble that was the Depression glass market collapsed. While many manufacturers tried to revive it, the marketplace never embraced it so enthusiastically again, until it became fashionable to "collect Depression glass" and the trend we know today as a secondary market started.

The era of collecting this beautiful glass blossomed quickly as collectors wanting to create a whole table service bought up bits and pieces. Many collectors specialized in one pattern or maker, or even one color; others chose to collect by form, such as creamers and sugars. As the secondary market expanded, price guides devoted to just that segment of the market began to appear. Weatherman's books were used as identification guides, but the new price guides developed by authors such as Carl F. Luckey, Kent Washburn, and Gene Florence began to establish a firm pricing tier.

Depression glass prices began to be traded by "book value" more and more until it was almost impossible to buy any Depression glass at all without paying established prices. Collectors and dealers were easily spotted at auctions and flea market as they scoured their favorite price guides to determine how much they could afford to pay and how much profit they could hope to achieve. A wonderful newspaper called *The Daze*, which was devoted to the Depression glass market, was founded by Nora Koch. Koch filled its pages with articles about patterns and companies, the activities of many collector clubs and show highlights, as well as print ads for Depression glass dealers all over the country. Sadly, when the Internet came roaring onto the scene, *The Daze* faded from the scene.

Today with the advent of online buying and more educated buyers, the Depression glass marketplace is beginning to level out and bargains can be found. Before the advent of the Internet, it was quite common to find pockets all across America where certain patterns were more prevalent and regional pricing was in effect. Today, the wide variations have pretty much disappeared.

Princess, green salad bowl, octagonal, **$55**; green cookie jar, **$85**.

Prices

The prices in *Depression Glass Warman's® Companion* have been established by carefully researching and compiling data from various sources, which include advertisements of glassware listed for sale in such publications as *Antique Trader Weekly*. Visits to auctions, antiques shops, malls, and flea markets yielded still another source of pricing data. Many specialized Depression-era glassware shows and general antiques shows were visited. The newest and probably most up-to-date pricing venue is the Internet. Several sites were visited daily to observe what patterns were being offered, as well as which colors seemed most popular and which forms were being sold.

Regional differences were noted and it seemed apparent that advertised prices were fairly constant. Of course, some patterns are more popular in certain areas, but there is no clear definition of what patterns are being collected by any particular geographic area—collectors remain individual in their tastes and preferences for certain patterns and colors.

Some colors in some patterns are just not being offered for sale in large enough quantities to get a true reading for the price structure. In those cases, a note as to availability has been included to guide the collector in establishing a value. The antiques and collectibles business is based on comparables, and great amounts of data must be analyzed to accurately evaluate pricing. Unlike many other aspects of the antiques and collectibles marketplace, Depression-

Newport, amethyst dinner plate, **$32**; cream soup bowl, **$25**; creamer, **$20**; and sugar, **$20**.

era glass is rarely sold at large specialized auctions; rather, collections are dispersed through dealers and to other collectors.

This is an area of the antiques and collectibles marketplace where developing a good relationship with reputable dealers is good. Many times dealers will retain "want lists" to help collectors fill in their patterns. And remember that although pricing for Depression-era glass has been driven by the major price guides for years, today the market is a buyer's market: expect to be able to pay less than "book value" if buying at auction, flea markets, etc. Bargains are out there, but it may take a little more searching to find interesting pieces at good prices.

Research

Depression-era glassware is one of the best-researched collecting areas available to the American marketplace. This is due in large part to the careful research of several people besides Weatherman, including Gene Florence, Carl F. Luckey, and Kent Washburn. Their volumes are held in high regard by researchers and collectors today. Many Depression-era glass collectors find their libraries grow as fast as their collections as they search to find what was manufactured in a particular pattern. By carefully researching company records and archives, these authors have allowed us to view what forms were popular, what colors delighted housewives of the era, and what sizes and shapes the patterns include.

Aurora, cobalt blue   bowl, **$20**; bowl, 4-1/2" d, **$85**; and milk pitcher, **$27.50**.

Reproductions

Reproductions of Depression-era glassware have greatly impacted the market. Whole patterns have fallen in value because collectors have become wary of investing in patterns beset by reproductions. Some patterns, like Miss America, are now experiencing reproductions of reproductions. The well-known clues to identifying the Miss America butter dish are now being compounded by having to recognize the second-generation reproduction and its identification clues.

Known reproductions, as of late 2006, are identified in the introduction of each pattern as well as being marked in the listing with †. Fantasy pieces, items not originally produced or produced in another color, are also listed as reproductions.

More detailed information on reproductions is included in the "Tips on Detecting Reproductions" chapter beginning on page 16. This excerpt is by Mark Chervenka, author of *Antique Trader™ Guide to Fakes and Reproductions*, 4th edition.

Collectors are encouraged to subscribe to *Antique and Collectors Reproduction News*, P.O. Box 71174, Des Moines, IA 50325. This excellent resource, available online at www.reponews.com, covers all areas of the antiques and collectibles marketplace, as well as Depression-era glassware.

REPRODUCTION! Mayfair Open Rose, green and blue cookie jars.

What's Included

This book includes patterns produced from 1920 through the 1960s. Such a wide time span allows patterns to be included from many manufacturers. The patterns selected reflect dinnerware patterns as opposed to elegant patterns or stemware-only patterns. To be included in this edition, a pattern had to meet several criteria:

· Be readily available on the marketplace
· Include a basic place setting, such as a cup and saucer, and plates
· Be manufactured during the time frame established
· Be manufactured in America
· Be eagerly sought by collectors

Very expensive items have been included in some patterns to give collectors a comparable value. Depression-era collectors are referred to other volumes that list rare and expensive Depression glass to firmly establish prices on those rare items. As in some other areas of the antiques and collectibles marketplace, rare does not always equate to a high dollar amount. And, some more readily found items command lofty prices because of high demand or other factors, not because they are necessarily rare. As collectors' tastes range from the simple patterns to the more elaborate ones, so does the ability of their budget to invest in inexpensive patterns to ones that cost hundreds of dollars per form.

To maintain the fine tradition of extensive descriptions typically found in Warman's® price guides, as much information as possible has been included as far as sizes, shapes, colors, etc. Whenever possible, the original manufacturer's language has been maintained, and a glossary is included to help you identify some of those puzzling names. As the patterns evolved, sometimes other names were assigned to pieces. Collectors and dealers today face the constant challenge of identifying not only the pattern, but also understanding the original

usage. It takes careful attention to detail to be able to discern the differences between berry, dessert, fruit, sauce, and cereal bowls. Color names are also given as the manufacturers originally named them.

The Depression-era glassware researchers have many accurate sources, including company records, catalogs, magazine advertisements, oral and written histories from sales staff, factory workers, etc. The dates included in the introductions are approximate, as are some of the factory locations. When companies had more than one factory, usually only the main office or factory is listed. With fine reference books available to collectors, *Depression Glass Warman's® Companion* concentrates on the pricing aspects of this segment of the antiques and collectibles market, rather than repeat the known company histories.

Forest Green, vase with original foil label, **$15**.

Today's Collectors

It has become quite evident that collectors of Depression-era glassware tend to use their treasures. Some collectors noted that they mix and match patterns, although most seem devoted to one color in a particular pattern. Sometimes colors will be mixed and matched as a collection is created for using. Often collectors later sell off those pieces that no longer match or go with their patterns. Many Depression-era glass collectors become dealers to support their habit and to reduce the strain on their groaning cupboards!

Depression glass has been identified as being one of the hottest areas of interest on the Internet. The ever-growing number of sites available to the serious collector and first-time buyer verifies this statement. Information about company histories, interesting articles, listings of shows, and shops is becoming more easily accessible as the World Wide Web gathers collectors together.

Purchasing Depression-era glassware via the Internet is a fun way to expand a collection, locate objects not normally found in a region, etc. However, care must be exercised when bidding or purchasing glassware online. Buyers should ask the seller the same questions online that they would when making a live purchase, such as the history of the piece, more details about the description, areas of damage, and return policy. Because there are hundreds of Depression-era patterns, sometimes items are misidentified, so a savvy collector must learn to recognize the intricacies of the pattern they are seeking.

Many Depression-era collectors consistently look to each other for support and knowledge. This is one area where the Internet has answered a need in that some collectors correspond or "chat" daily at online message boards and forums about their collections, sharing experiences and dreams. During Depression

glass antiques shows, it is not uncommon to see dealers and collectors offering their opinion about the source of a particular piece, what colors are available, etc. Perhaps this helps explain why so many young collectors are drawn to this colorful glassware: Information is readily available, standard price guides are used to establish prices, and knowledge is freely shared. Add to that excellent reference books, and you have an ever-increasing pool of collectors. Many exciting treasures await those who actively search for the rainbow of sparkling colors known today as Depression-era glass.

Hobnail, pink sherbet, **$10**.

Thanks

Artist Jerry O'Brien produced the superb line drawings accompanying each pattern. Whenever possible, he worked from an actual example, measuring details and analyzing the pattern from an artist's point of view. Sometimes an actual plate, saucer, or other piece was photocopied and the lines meticulously traced and enhanced to show details. Geometric patterns were reproduced using more technical drawing skills. Where the pattern repeats evenly around the piece, only a portion is shown, allowing more room for pertinent information. In other patterns, such as Parrot (Sylvan), the whole pattern is shown so collectors can see the relative location of the parrots, foliage, etc.

To facilitate the photography of all these beautiful patterns, several Depression-era dealers and private collectors generously loaned us pieces. Each piece was hand selected for the book, told to smile, carefully washed, and wrapped for transport. Those who deserve our thanks for this task include Rick Hirte, Fran Jay, Tony and Jeanne Jacobsen, Mildred McCurdy, Neil McCurdy, Al and Rubie Myers, Pam and Nick Ochs, and Troy Vozzella. Photographer Donna Chiarelli carefully positioned the pieces, adjusting lights and cameras to present each one's best side! Also, thanks to James Hintz and Tina Trautman for their photography contributions.

In addition, support and guidance has been terrific and freely given by many. Through daily chats online, e-mails, conversations, and letters, I have received encouragement and guidance. Add to that an understanding family willing to pitch in. To all those, I say thanks!

And, most important, thanks to you, the collectors, dealers, and those who read books such as *Depression Glass Warman's® Companion*, for it is all of you who keep the Depression glass market glittering.

Patrician, back, from left: amber tumbler, 9 oz, 4-1/4" h, **$32**; cup and saucer, **$10**. Front, from left: amber luncheon plate, 9" d, **$14**; dinner plate, 10-1/2" d, **$10**; and salad plate, 7-1/2" d, **$17.50**.

Tips on Detecting Reproductions

From *Antique Trader™ Guide to Fakes and Reproductions*, 4th edition by Mark Chervenka. Used with permission.

Depression glass has been widely reproduced since the 1970s. Reproductions include rare patterns and colors such as Royal Lace in cobalt blue as well as everyday standards such as pink Cherry Blossom.

The most reliable way to catch reproductions is to compare details in the molded pattern. Unfortunately, there is no one single test that can be used across all the patterns, colors, and shapes. Eliminating the fakes is pretty much a piece-by-piece process, requiring comparisons to the originals you'll find in the following pages.

That said, here are some very broad rules of thumb about Depression glass reproductions.

• Almost all new pieces feel slick or greasy to the touch due to a high sodium content in the glass formula that attracts moisture and dust.

• Many pieces will not function for the purpose they were supposedly created. New spouts often don't pour correctly. Knobs and handles, like those on pitchers and butter dish lids, can be difficult to grasp.

• Color alone is not a good test of age. Colors change with the glass batch. The best test is to compare molded details.

• Some new glass has a strong vinegar-like odor.

It is very important to apply guidelines to only the particular piece of a pattern piece being discussed. For example, don't assume the test for tumblers is the same test you would use for shakers. Don't assume a particular test described for a piece in one pattern can be used for a similarly shaped piece in any other pattern.

There are many more reproductions than those listed in these pages. Pieces for this section were chosen because they are either so widespread almost everyone will encounter them or are very similar to originals and harder to detect. Patterns are listed alphabetically with the various shapes listed separately under the pattern name.

■ Cherry Blossom

Original: Jeanette Glass Co., 1930s.

Reproductions: Reproductions have been on the market since 1973. The majority of new pieces have been made in Japan, Taiwan, and China. New colors include pink, green, red, transparent blue, Delphite, cobalt blue, and a variety of iridized (carnival) finishes.

Reproduction Cherry Blossom has been made or is being made in the following known shapes:

berry bowls, 8-1/2" and 4-3/4"
butter dish, covered
cake plate (on three feet)
cereal bowl, 5-3/4"
child/toy sizes in cup, saucer, butter, sugar, and creamer
cup and saucer
pitcher, 36-ounce all over pattern (AOP), scalloped foot
plate, 9" dinner
shakers
platter, 13", divided
tray, 10-1/2", two-handled, sandwich
tumbler, all over pattern (AOP), scalloped foot

As a general rule, most Cherry Blossom reproductions can be identified by crudely shaped cherries and leaves. Old leaves have a realistic appearance with serrated (sawtooth) edges and veins that vary in length and thickness. New leaves commonly have perfectly straight and uniformly even veins that form V-shaped grooves. Original cherries usually give an illusion of a rounded three-dimensional ball-shaped figure; many new cherries appear to be only a flat circle. Differences between old and new patterns are generally greater in earlier 1970s reproductions than in more recent reproductions.

Most original Cherry Blossom in green glass fluoresces under long wave black light. This is not a positive test for age, though, because several green reproductions also fluoresce. This includes a new butter dish, new tumbler, new cup, and several other shapes. While a black light is useful, don't rely on it as your only test of age.

Original Cherry Blossom leaves look real. They have irregular sawtooth edges and both large and small veins. Reproduction leaves usually have smooth or feathery edges. New veins are generally straight-sided V-shaped grooves or regularly spaced lines.

New leaves

serrated edges

veins of different length & thickness

Old leaf

First reproduction base has unrealistic flat cherries and fishbone-type veins in leaves.

Second reproduction base has improved pattern, but note that the branch stops short of the rim.

Original lid has two lines around bottom rim of lid. Original base has realistic cherries and leaves; the branch touches both sides of the rim.

Pattern detail of a typical new cup. The blossoms don't touch the ends of the twigs, and the leaves do not appear natural.

Pattern detail of a typical original cup. Note that the blossoms and twigs touch, and the leaves look natural and realistic.

BUTTER DISH (COVERED)

Child/Toy Size: This is a fantasy item; no original child's butter dish was ever made. All pieces now on the market are new.

Full Size: There are at least two styles of reproductions. The 1970s reproduction has a very crude pattern in the base. A later reproduction has an improved pattern in the base, but the branch stops short of the rim. The original base has realistic leaves and cherries with a branch that extends from rim to rim.

All reproduction lids made so far have a smooth band separated from the rest of the lid by a single line. On old lids, the band is separated by two lines.

All reproduction lids made so far have a smooth band separated from the rest of the lid by a single line. On old lids, the band is separated by two lines.

CUP

The pattern in old cups is very realistic. Each old twig ends in a blossom with the twig touching the blossom. In new cups, there is an obvious gap between the blossom and the twig. In old cups, the pattern fills almost the entire bottom; in new cups, the pattern is faint and weak. Leaves on old cups look like leaves; leaves on the new cups look like arrowheads or barbs.

PITCHER

The all over pattern (AOP) scallop-foot pitcher has been reproduced since the 1970s. The easiest way to tell old from new pitchers is to turn the

Far left: The base of new AOP pitchers have crude leaves with unnatural V-shaped veins in leaves. Only seven cherries are visible in the base of new pitchers.

Left: Nine cherries are visible in the pattern on bases of original AOP pitchers. Leaves and cherries are well molded and natural in appearance.

pitcher over and look at the design on the bottom. Now, count the cherries. Old pitchers have nine cherries; new pitchers have only seven cherries. The arrangement of leaves and cherries on the bases of new pitchers is poorly designed with lots of open space in the pattern. Leaves and cherries on the bases of original pitchers are realistic and the pattern covers almost the entire bottom.

TUMBLER

New and old tumblers have been reproduced since the 1970s and can be distinguished by the pattern on the base. The cherries and leaves in the bases of original tumblers are sharp and well defined. The pattern nearly fills the entire concave space of original tumblers. There are at least two reproductions of AOP tumblers. Both have poorly molded details with unrealistic cherries and leaves. In both new tumblers, the pattern is primarily in the concave center with lots of space between the pattern and the flat rim. You can also separate old and new tumblers by the molded horizontal lines around the smooth band in the top rim. Old tumblers have three horizontal lines; new tumblers only one. The three molded lines on original tumblers are sharp and strong.

New tumbler, Style A. This style was introduced in the mid-1970s and continued to be made through the 1990s. The design in the foot has the typical new leaves and cherries. The pattern in the foot is mostly in the center with lots of open space around the edge of the foot.

New tumbler, Style B. The design on the foot is very weak and usually found in the very center only. This style was made in pink, green, and Delphite Blue. New Style B was made around 1980 and, when it first came out, H.M. Weatherman reported it in *Price Trends 1981*.

Original tumbler. The design in the foot is sharp and almost fills the entire base; the leaves and cherries are natural and realistic.

Floral (Poinsettia)

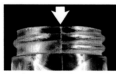

In new shakers, the threads run in an unbroken continuous line across the mold seam.

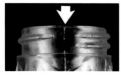

In old shakers, there is a 1/4" gap in the threads as they cross the mold seam.

Original: Jeannette Glass Co., 1931 to 1935. Original colors include amber, crystal, Delphite, green, pink, red, and yellow.

Reproductions: New shakers are appearing in cobalt blue, dark green, pink, and red. Shakers in cobalt blue, dark green, and red are obvious reproductions because those colors were never used in original production. The new pink shakers, however, are very close in color and pattern to the originals.

SHAKER

The quickest test for separating new and old shakers is to examine the molded glass threads. In old shakers, there is a 1/4" horizontal gap between the raised threads along the mold seam. No thread goes over the mold seam on old shakers. In the new shakers, threads are continuous, and there is no gap at the mold seam. New shakers also tend to have more glass at the bottom, but this can be hard to measure and may vary slightly. Checking the threads is a more reliable way to identify the new pieces.

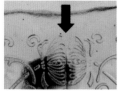

In the new pitcher, the pattern stops and starts at the mold seam under the pour spout.

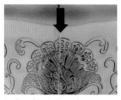

In the old pitcher, the pattern is split by the mold seam under the pour spout.

Florentine #2 (Poppy #2)

Original: Hazel Atlas Glass Co., 1932 to 1935.
Reproductions: Cone-footed 7-1/2" pitcher and 4" footed tumbler. New colors include a blue that is often mistaken for the rarest original color, which is ice blue.

The center of the bases in new tumblers (left) is plain without a pattern. The pattern is included in the bases of old tumblers (right).

Madrid

Original: Federal Glass Co., 1932 to 1939.

Reproductions: There are two groups of modern Madrid. In 1976, Federal changed the pattern name to Recollection and began making new pieces. The first new pieces of Recollection were easily identified because pieces were dated in the mold with the year "1976." But then, Federal Glass went bankrupt, and the rights to the design were acquired by Indiana Glass. Indiana Glass discontinued dating the glass and that has caused problems for collectors. So far, new pieces have been made in five colors: amber, blue, clear, pink, and teal. Teal, a greenish-blue, almost aqua color, is the only new color not originally made. The other four colors—amber, pink, blue, and clear—were all used for the 1930s Madrid.

The situation is further confused because Indiana Glass has also introduced many shapes never originally made, such as the cake stand, goblet, covered candy dish, and others. Don't mistake these items for rare or unlisted pieces just because you can't find them in a book.

Known shapes reproduced to date include: covered butter dish, dinner plate, grill plate, luncheon plate, creamer, open sugar, shaker, cup, saucer, goblet*, vase*, hurricane lamp*, pedestal covered candy dish*, footed cake stand*, footed fruit stand/dish*, 9-1/2" bowl, 10" oval vegetable bowl, 7" soup/cereal bowl, and candleholder. Items marked with an asterisk* are shapes never made in original 1930s Madrid.

The original Madrid pattern was renamed "Recollection" and marketed by Indiana Glass Co. Many new shapes are similar to the original 1930s Madrid, including the butter dish shown here in the new Recollection box.

New covered candy dish (left); new footed goblet (right). Neither shape was made in the original 1930s Madrid.

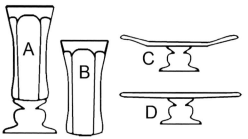

Shaker

New   Old

New shapes not made in original 1930s Madrid: A. "hurricane lamp" made by attaching candleholder to tumbler; B. tumbler; C. fruit stand made by joining candleholder to dinner plate; D. cake stand, same as C. but with flat edges.

The new shaker is a squat barrel-shape. There are two styles of old shakers. Both old shakers are slender, vertical shapes: one is footed, the other has a flat bottom.

Butter Dish

Far left: The mold seam in the knob on the new butter dish lid has a vertical mold seam.
Left: he mold seam on the old butter dish knob is horizontal.

Cup and Sugar Bowl

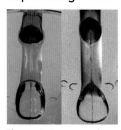

The easiest way to detect new cups and new sugars is to examine how their handles join the bodies. Looking at the inside of a sugar bowl or cup, the lower part of old handles (right) forms a tear drop shape. The same area in new handles form an oval (left).

Creamer

Spouts on new creamers rise above the top rim.

Spouts on new creamers do not rise above the top rim.

◼ Royal Lace

Original: Hazel Atlas, 1934 to 1941.

Reproductions: Cookie jar, 9 ounce tumbler, and 5 ounce juice glass. The majority of new tumblers are cobalt blue. Cookie jars are produced in a variety of colors.

Cookie Jar

Pay particular attention to lids, as they are the most valuable part of the cookie jar. Genuine old jars are easier to find than old lids, so be alert for new lids on old jars. All old lids have a single mold seam that splits the lid in half. There is no mold seam on the new lids.

New Royal Lace cookie jar.

The bottom of the base of the new cookie jar is smooth and plain.

The bottom of the base of the old cookie jar has a molded circular plunger mark.

Tumbler

The glass in the sides and bottoms of both sizes of new tumblers is generally about two to three times as thick as originals.

Old 5 ounce juice glasses have a geometric design molded in the bottom (far left). Bottoms of new 5 ounce juice glasses are plain with no pattern (left).

◼ Sharon (Cabbage Rose)

Original: Federal Glass Co., 1935 to 1939.

Reproductions: Includes covered butter dish, candy jar, cheese dish, shakers, and sugar and creamer.

Butter Dish

The best test for lids is to examine the knob. On old lids there is only about 1/4" between the bottom of the old knob and the top of the lid. It's very hard to get your fingers under the knob of an original lid. The gap under the knobs on new lids is about 1/2".

An original Sharon butter dish. New and old can be separated by the knob on the lid.

There is a much larger gap under the knobs of new lids. The gap under the knob in new lids is about 1/2". The space under the old knob is 1/4".

Sugar and Creamer

◯or◯ ◇or◇
how handles
join sugar and creamer bowls
as seen from inside

If you look inside the bowls of sugars and creamers, you'll see a difference between how handles join the body. In new sugars and creamers, the area where handles join the body form a circle or very rounded oval (left). The same area in the original sugar and creamer forms a pointed oval or teardrop shape.

Candy Jar

The new Sharon candy jar (left), is very similar to the original (right).

The foot on the new base (top) is only about 2-7/8" diameter. The foot on the original base (bottom) is 3-1/4" in diameter.

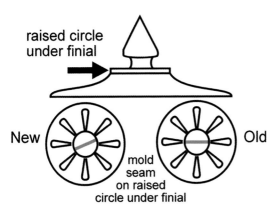

raised circle under finial

New

Old

mold seam on raised circle under finial

You can separate new and old lids by the location of the mold seam, shown in red, on the raised disc under the finial. When you look down at the circle from above, the mold seam on old lids is aligned with two raised ribs. The mold seam in the new lid appears between two raised ribs.

Thumbnail Guide

Depression-era glassware can be confusing. Many times when a manufacturer created a successful new design, other companies immediately produced similar patterns. The following quick identification guide classifies patterns by design elements. Compare your piece with the drawings to find the matching design, and then consult the detailed pattern listing and larger drawing for more information. Note: This thumbnail guide includes more patterns than those listed in the main body of the book.

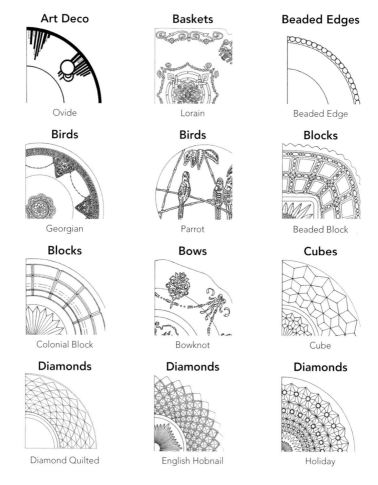

Art Deco	Baskets	Beaded Edges
Ovide	Lorain	Beaded Edge

Birds	Birds	Blocks
Georgian	Parrot	Beaded Block

Blocks	Bows	Cubes
Colonial Block	Bowknot	Cube

Diamonds	Diamonds	Diamonds
Diamond Quilted	English Hobnail	Holiday

Diamonds

Laced Edge

Diamonds

Miss America

Diamonds

Waterford

Diamonds

Windsor

Ellipses

Newport

Florals

Cherry Blossom

Florals

Cloverleaf

Florals

Daisy

Florals

Dogwood

Florals

Doric

Florals

Doric & Pansy

Florals

Floragold

Florals

Floral & Diamond Band

Florals

Indiana Custard

Geometric/Line

Floral

Florals

Iris

Florals

Jubilee

Florals

Mayfair (Federal)

Florals

Mayfair (Open Rose)

Florals

Normandie

Florals

Pineapple & Floral

Florals

Rosemary

Florals

Rose Cameo

Florals

Royal Lace

Florals

Sharon

Florals

Sunflower

Florals

Thistle

Figures

Cameo

Fruit

Fruits

Geometric/Line

Wexford

Geometric/Line

Constellation

Geometric/Line

Cracked Ice

Geometric/Line

Early American Prescut

Geometric/Line

Park Avenue

Geometric/Line

Pioneer

Geometric/Line

Sierra

Geometric/Line

Star

Geometric/Line

Tea Room

Honeycomb

Aunt Polly

Honeycomb

Hex Optic

Horseshoe

Horseshoe

Lacy Designs

Harp

Lacy Designs

Heritage

Lacy Designs

Sandwich (Hocking)

Leaves

Sunburst

Loops

Christmas Candy

Loops

Old Colony

Loops

Pretzel

Petals

Aurora

Petals

Circle

Petals

Colonial

Petals

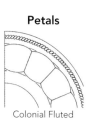

Colonial Fluted

Petals

National

Petals

New Century

Petals

Old Café

Petals

Ribbon

Petals

Roulette

Petals

Victory

Petals/Ridges

Anniversary

Petals/Ridges

Coronation

Petals/Ridges

Fortune

Petals/Ridges

Petalware

Petals/Ridges

Queen Mary

Plain

Mt. Pleasant

Pyramids

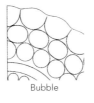

Pyramid

Raised Bands

Forest Green

Raised Bands

Royal Ruby

Raised Circles

Bubble

Raised Circles

Columbia

Raised Circles

Dewdrop

Raised Circles

Hobnail

Raised Circles

Moonstone

Raised Circles

Oyster & Pearl

Raised Circles

Raindrops

Raised Circles

Radiance

Raised Circles

Ships

Raised Circles

Thumbprint

Raised Circles

Yorktown

Ribs

Homespun

Rings

Manhattan

Rings

Moderntone

Rings

Moondrops

Rings

Moroccan Amethyst

Rings

Old English

Rings

Ring

Scrolling Designs

Adam

Scrolling Designs

American Sweetheart

Scrolling Designs

Florentine No. 1

Scrolling Designs

Florentine No. 2

Scrolling Designs

Madrid

Scrolling Designs

Patrician

Scrolling Designs

Patrick

Scrolling Designs

Princess

Scrolling Designs

Vernon

Swirls

Diana

Swirls

Ripple

Swirls

Swirl

Swirls

Twisted Optic

Swirls

U.S. Swirl

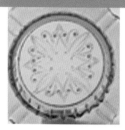

Adam

Manufactured by Jeannette Glass Company, Jeannette, Pa., from 1932 to 1934.

Pieces are made in crystal, Delphite blue, green, pink, some topaz and yellow. Delphite 4-inch high candlesticks are valued at $250 a pair. A yellow cup and saucer are valued at $200, and a 7-3/4-inch diameter yellow plate is valued at $115. Production in topaz and yellow was limited. Crystal prices are approximately 50 percent of the prices listed for green.

Reproductions: † Butter dish in pink and green.

Item	Green	Pink
Ashtray, 4-1/2" d	28.00	30.00
Berry bowl, small	22.50	18.50
Bowl, 9" d, cov	90.00	75.00
Bowl, 9" d, open	45.00	30.00
Bowl, 10" l, oval	40.00	40.00
Butter dish, cov †	395.00	135.00
Cake plate, 10" d, ftd	38.00	40.00
Candlesticks, pr, 4" h	125.00	100.00
Candy jar, cov, 2-1/2" h	120.00	135.00
Casserole, cov	95.00	80.00
Cereal bowl, 5-3/4" d	50.00	40.00
Coaster, 3-1/4" d	32.00	35.00
Creamer	30.00	35.00
Cup	30.00	28.00
Dessert bowl, 4-3/4" d	25.00	25.00
Iced tea tumbler, 5-1/2" h	72.00	75.00
Lamp	500.00	500.00
Pitcher, 32 oz, round base	—	125.00
Pitcher, 32 oz, 8" h	48.00	45.00
Plate, 6" d, sherbet	15.00	18.00
Plate, 7-3/4" d, salad, sq	18.50	19.50
Plate, 9" d, dinner, sq	37.50	42.00
Plate, 9" d, grill	37.50	35.00
Platter, 11-3/4" l, rect	38.00	38.00
Relish dish, 8" l, divided	27.00	20.00
Salt and pepper shakers, pr, 4" h	130.00	95.00
Saucer, 6" sq	12.00	10.00
Sherbet, 3"	40.00	38.00
Sugar, cov	48.00	65.00
Tumbler, 4-1/2" h	35.00	40.00
Vase, 7-1/2" h	60.00	550.00
Vegetable bowl, cov, 7-3/4" d	95.00	75.00
Vegetable bowl, open, 7-3/4" d	30.00	40.00

Far left: Adam, green ashtray, **$45**; pink pitcher, **$28.**

Left: Adam, green plate, **$18.50.**

American Sweetheart

Manufactured by Macbeth-Evans Glass Company, Charleroi, Pa., from 1930 to 1936.

Pieces are made in blue, Monax, pink, and red. There is limited production in Cremax and color-trimmed Monax.

Item	Blue	Cremax	Monax	Monax w/Color Trim	Pink	Red
Berry bowl, 3-1/4" d, flat	—	—	—	—	90.00	—
Berry bowl, 9" d	—	140.00	85.00	200.00	75.00	—
Cereal bowl, 6" d	—	19.50	20.00	50.00	28.00	—
Chop plate, 11" d	—	—	26.00	—	—	—
Console bowl, 18" d	1,450.00	—	550.00	—	—	1,200.00
Cream soup, 4-1/2" d	—	—	135.00	—	100.00	—
Creamer, ftd	195.00	—	15.00	110.00	20.00	175.00
Cup	160.00	—	15.00	100.00	20.00	95.00
Lamp shade	—	450.00	995.00	—	—	—
Pitcher, 60 oz, 7-1/2" h	—	—	—	—	995.00	—
Pitcher, 80 oz, 8" h	—	—	—	—	795.00	—
Plate, 6" d, bread and butter	—	—	7.50	24.00	10.00	—
Plate, 8" d, salad	135.00	—	12.00	30.00	15.00	145.00
Plate, 9" d, luncheon	—	—	19.50	48.00	—	—
Plate, 9-3/4" d, dinner	—	—	25.00	90.00	45.00	—
Plate, 10-1/4" d, dinner	—	—	30.00	—	45.00	—
Platter, 13" l, oval	—	—	85.00	225.00	75.00	—
Salt and pepper shakers, pr, ftd	—	—	395.00	—	500.00	—
Salver plate, 12" d	275.00	—	30.00	—	30.00	200.00
Saucer	25.00	—	7.00	18.00	7.50	45.00
Serving plate, 15-1/2" d	450.00	—	250.00	—	—	350.00
Sherbet, 3-3/4" h, ftd	—	—	25.00	—	30.00	—
Sherbet, 4-1/4" h, ftd	—	—	25.00	110.00	25.00	—
Soup bowl, flat, 9-1/2" d	—	—	95.00	170.00	85.00	—
Sugar, open, ftd	195.00	—	15.00	110.00	15.00	175.00
Tidbit, two-tier	350.00	—	95.00	—	250.00	—
Tidbit, three-tier	750.00	—	275.00	—	—	600.00
Tumbler, 5 oz, 3-1/2" h	—	—	—	—	130.00	—
Tumbler, 9 oz, 4-1/4" h	—	—	—	—	95.00	—
Tumbler, 10 oz, 4-3/4" h	—	—	—	—	185.00	—
Vegetable bowl, 11"	—	—	90.00	—	85.00	—

Far left: American Sweetheart, Monax dinner plate, 10-1/4" d, **$30.**

Left: American Sweetheart, Monax open sugar, **$15**; and creamer, **$11.50.**

Anniversary

Manufactured by Jeannette Glass Company, Jeannette, Pa., from 1947 to 1949, late 1960s to mid-1970s.

Pieces are made in crystal, iridescent, and pink.

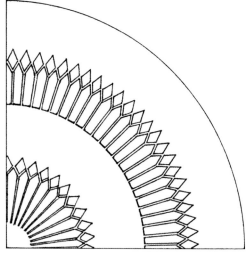

Item	Crystal	Iridescent	Pink
Berry bowl, 4-7/8" d	6.50	5.50	12.00
Butter dish, cov	25.00	—	50.00
Cake plate, 12-3/8" w, square	7.00	—	16.50
Cake plate, 12-1/2" d, round	18.00	—	18.50
Cake plate, metal cover	15.00	—	—
Candlesticks, pr, 4-7/8" h	20.00	25.00	—
Candy jar, cov	24.00	—	45.00
Comport, open, three legs	5.00	5.00	16.00
Comport, ruffled, three legs	6.50	—	—
Creamer, ftd	6.00	6.50	14.00
Cup	5.00	4.00	9.00
Fruit bowl, 9" d	15.00	14.50	24.50
Pickle, 9" d	5.50	7.50	12.00
Plate, 6-1/4" d, sherbet	2.00	3.50	4.00
Plate, 9" d, dinner	8.00	8.50	18.00
Plate, 10" d, dinner	15.00	—	—
Relish dish, 8" d	10.00	12.50	16.00
Sandwich server, 12-1/2" d	6.50	10.00	20.00
Saucer	1.00	1.50	6.00
Sherbet, ftd	10.00	—	12.00
Soup bowl, 7-3/8" d	8.00	7.50	18.00
Sugar, cov	12.00	10.00	20.00
Sugar, open, gold trim	4.50	—	—
Tidbit, metal handle	14.00	—	—
Vase, 6-1/2" h	20.00	—	30.00
Wall pocket	65.00	—	90.00
Wine, 2-1/2 oz	12.00	—	25.00

Anniversary, iridescent dinner plate, **$8.**

Aunt Polly

Manufactured by U.S. Glass Company, Pittsburgh, Pa., in the late 1920s.

Pieces are made in blue, green, and iridescent.

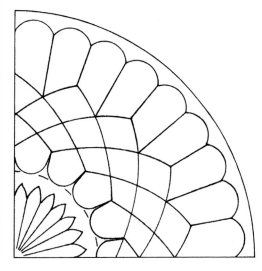

Item	Blue	Green	Iridescent
Berry bowl, 4-3/4" d, individual	20.00	15.00	15.00
Berry bowl, 7-1/8" d, master	45.00	22.00	22.00
Bowl, 4-3/4" d, 2" h	—	15.00	15.00
Bowl, 5-1/2" d, one handle	25.00	15.00	15.00
Bowl, 8-3/8" l, oval	100.00	42.00	42.00
Butter dish, cov	225.00	210.00	200.00
Candy jar, cov, two handles	50.00	30.00	30.00
Candy jar, ftd, two handles	—	27.50	27.50
Creamer	60.00	32.00	32.00
Pickle, 7-1/4" l, oval, handle	45.00	20.00	20.00
Pitcher, 48 oz, 8" h	200.00	—	—
Plate, 6" d, sherbet	16.00	6.00	6.00
Plate, 8" d, luncheon	20.00	—	—
Salt and pepper shakers, pr	245.00	—	—
Sherbet	15.00	12.00	12.00
Sugar	195.00	95.00	95.00
Tumbler, 8 oz, 3-5/8" h	35.00	—	—
Vase, 6-1/2" h, ftd	55.00	35.00	38.00

Aunt Polly, blue sherbet, **$15.**

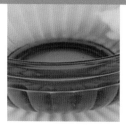

Aurora

Manufactured by Hazel Atlas Glass Company, Clarksburg, West Virginia, and Zanesville, Ohio, in the late 1930s.

Pieces are made in cobalt (Ritz) blue, crystal, green, and pink.

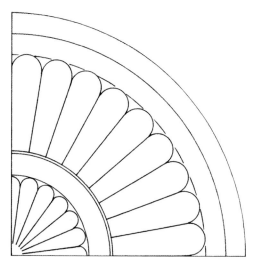

Item	Cobalt Blue	Crystal	Green	Pink
Bowl, 4-1/2" d	85.00	—	—	75.00
Breakfast set, 24 pcs, service for four	500.00	—	—	—
Cereal bowl, 5-3/8" d	20.00	12.00	9.50	15.00
Cup	20.00	6.00	10.0	15.00
Milk pitcher	27.50	—	—	25.00
Plate, 6-1/2" d	12.50	—	—	12.50
Saucer	7.50	2.00	3.00	6.00
Tumbler, 10 oz, 4-3/4" h	32.50	—	—	35.50

Aurora, cobalt blue cereal bowl, **$20**; bowl, 4-1/2" d, **$85**.

Aurora, cobalt blue milk pitcher, **$27.50.**

Beaded Block

Manufactured by Imperial Glass Company, Bellaire, Ohio, from 1927 to the 1930s.

Pieces are made in amber, crystal, green, ice blue, iridescent, milk white (1950s), opalescent, pink, red, and Vaseline. Some pieces are still being made in pink and are embossed with the "IG" trademark. The only form known in red is the 4-1/2-inch lily bowl, valued at $300. The secondary market for milk white is still being established.

Item	Amber	Crystal	Green	Ice Blue
Bowl, 4-1/2" d, lily	22.00	18.00	20.00	26.00
Bowl, 4-1/2" d, two handles	18.00	10.00	22.00	28.00
Bowl, 5-1/2" sq	18.00	8.00	20.00	12.00
Bowl, 5-1/2" d, one handle	18.00	8.00	20.00	12.00
Bowl, 6" deep	24.00	12.00	24.00	15.00
Bowl, 6-1/4" d	24.00	8.50	20.00	12.00
Bowl, 6-1/2" d, two handles	24.00	8.50	20.00	12.00
Bowl, 6-3/4" d	27.50	12.00	28.00	14.00
Bowl, 7-1/4" d, flared	30.00	12.00	28.00	14.00
Bowl, 7-1/2" d, fluted	30.00	22.00	30.00	24.00
Bowl, 7-1/2", plain	30.00	20.00	30.00	22.00
Candy dish, cov, pear shaped	—	—	395.00	—
Celery, 8-1/4" d	35.00	18.00	35.00	18.00
Creamer, ftd	25.00	25.00	25.00	24.00
Jelly, 4-1/2" h, stemmed	20.00	10.00	20.00	12.00
Jelly, 4-1/2" h, stemmed, flared lid	24.00	20.00	24.00	30.00
Pitcher, one pt, 5-1/4" h	95.00	115.00	125.00	115.00
Plate, 7-3/4" sq	20.00	7.50	20.00	10.00
Plate, 8-3/4"	30.00	24.00	30.00	30.00
Sugar, ftd	25.00	24.00	30.00	30.00
Syrup	—	—	—	—
Vase, 6" h, ftd	25.00	20.00	35.00	35.00

Item	Iridescent	Opal	Pink	Vaseline
Bowl, 4-1/2" d, lily	18.00	30.00	18.00	24.00
Bowl, 4-1/2" d, two handles	20.00	30.00	12.00	28.00
Bowl, 5-1/2" sq	10.00	15.00	10.00	12.00
Bowl, 5-1/2" d, one handle	10.00	15.00	20.00	12.00
Bowl, 6" deep	12.00	24.00	18.00	15.00
Bowl, 6-1/4" d	12.00	18.00	10.00	12.00
Bowl, 6-1/2" d, two handles	12.00	18.00	28.00	12.00
Bowl, 6-3/4" d	15.00	20.00	14.00	14.00
Bowl, 7-1/4" d, flared	15.00	20.00	14.00	14.00
Bowl, 7-1/2" d, fluted	20.00	24.00	24.00	24.00
Bowl, 7-1/2", plain	24.00	24.00	20.00	22.00
Candy dish, cov, pear shaped	—	—	—	650.00
Celery, 8-1/4" d	18.00	30.00	16.50	18.00
Creamer, ftd	24.00	50.00	30.00	24.00
Jelly, 4-1/2" h, stemmed	12.00	15.00	12.00	12.00
Jelly, 4-1/2" h, stemmed, flared lid	15.00	24.00	15.00	12.00
Pitcher, one pt, 5-1/4" h	115.00	125.00	195.00	115.00
Plate, 7-3/4" sq	10.00	15.00	8.00	10.00
Plate, 8-3/4"	20.00	24.00	20.00	20.00
Sugar, ftd	20.00	60.00	30.00	20.00
Syrup	—	—	—	165.00
Vase, 6" h, ftd	25.00	20.00	36.00	30.00

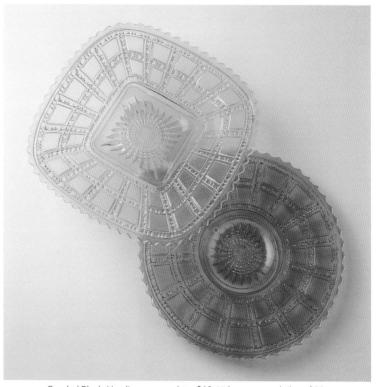

Beaded Block, Vaseline square plate, **$10**; iridescent round plate, **$20.**

Beaded Block, ice blue vase, **$35**; crystal jelly, stemmed, **$10.**

Beaded Edge

Pattern #22 Milk Glass

Made by Westmoreland Glass Co., late 1930s-1950s.

Pieces are made in white milk glass. Painted decorations add interesting variety to this pattern. Collectors can find eight different fruit patterns and eight different floral patterns; others include birds and Christmas designs. Another variation incorporates a red edge or band into the design.

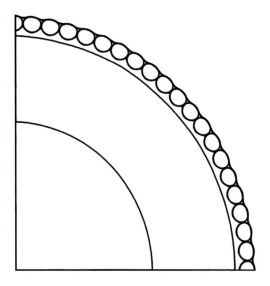

Item	Decorated	Plain	Red Edge
Creamer, cov, ftd	35.00	20.00	25.00
Creamer, open, ftd	18.00	10.00	14.00
Cup	12.00	5.00	6.50
Nappy, 5" d	16.00	4.50	10.00
Nappy, 6" d, crimped	22.00	7.50	12.00
Plate, 6" d, bread and butter	19.00	5.00	7.00
Plate, 7" d, salad	15.00	8.00	9.00
Plate, 7-1/2" d, coupe	15.00	10.00	12.00
Plate, 8-1/2" d, luncheon	25.00	8.50	10.00
Plate, 10-1/2" d, dinner	45.00	12.00	20.00
Platter, 12" l, tab handles	90.00	75.00	45.00
Relish, three-part	90.00	25.00	50.00
Salt and pepper shakers, pr	75.00	30.00	35.00
Saucer	5.00	2.00	2.50
Sherbet, ftd	18.00	8.50	12.00
Sugar, cov, ftd	35.00	20.00	25.00
Sugar, open, ftd	18.00	10.00	14.00
Torte plate, 15" d	70.00	25.00	40.00
Tumbler, ftd, 8 oz	15.00	10.00	15.00

Beaded Edge, white luncheon plate, **$8.50.**

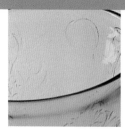

Bowknot

Unknown maker, late 1920s.

Pieces are made in green.

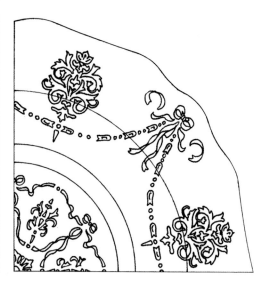

Item	Green
Berry bowl, 4-1/2" d	25.00
Cereal bowl, 5-1/2" d	30.00
Cup	20.00
Plate, 7" d, salad	18.00
Sherbet, low, ftd	25.00
Tumbler, 10 oz, 5" h, flat	20.00
Tumbler, 10 oz, 5" h, ftd	25.00

Bowknot, green tumbler, **$12.**

Bowknot, footed berry bowl, **$25.**

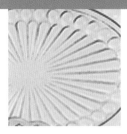

Bubble

Bullseye, Provincial

Manufactured originally by Hocking Glass Company, and followed by Anchor Hocking Glass Corporation, Lancaster, Ohio, from 1937 to 1965.

Pieces are made in crystal (1937); forest green (1937); pink, Royal Ruby (1963); and sapphire blue (1937). Production in pink was limited. The current value for a pink cup and saucer is $175.

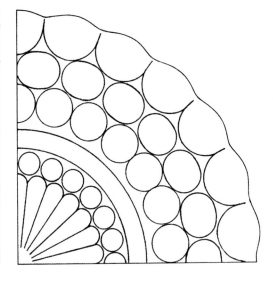

Item	Crystal	Forest Green	Royal Ruby	Sapphire Blue
Berry bowl, 4" d	4.00	—	6.50	20.00
Berry bowl, 8-3/4" d	12.00	15.00	15.00	20.00
Bowl, 9" d, flanged	8.00	—	—	335.00
Candlesticks, pr	18.00	40.00	—	—
Cereal bowl, 5-1/4" d	10.00	20.00	—	17.50
Cocktail, 3-1/2 oz	4.50	15.00	18.00	—
Cocktail, 4-1/2 oz	4.50	16.00	16.00	—
Creamer	7.50	15.00	18.00	45.00
Cup	4.50	9.75	12.50	15.00
Fruit bowl, 4-1/2" d	5.00	11.00	9.00	12.00
Goblet, 9 oz, stem, 5-1/2" h	7.50	15.00	15.00	—
Goblet, 9-1/2 oz, stem	8.00	15.00	18.00	—
Goblet, 10-3/4 oz, 5-3/8" h	—	14.50	—	—
Iced tea goblet, 14 oz	8.00	17.50	—	—
Iced tea tumbler, 12 oz, 4-1/2" h	12.50	—	19.50	—
Juice goblet, 4 oz	3.00	14.00	—	—
Juice goblet, 5-1/2 oz	5.00	12.50	15.00	—
Juice tumbler, 6 oz, ftd	4.00	12.00	10.00	—
Lamp, three styles	42.00	—	—	—
Lemonade tumbler, 16 oz, 5-7/8" h	16.00	—	16.00	—
Old fashioned tumbler, 8 oz, 3-1/4" h	6.50	16.00	16.50	—
Pitcher, 64 oz, ice lip	60.00	—	65.00	—
Plate, 6-3/4" d, bread and butter	4.00	4.50	—	3.75
Plate, 9-3/8" d, dinner	7.50	28.00	27.50	10.00
Plate, 9-3/8" d, grill	—	20.00	—	22.00
Platter, 12" l, oval	10.00	—	—	18.00
Sandwich plate, 9-1/2" d	7.50	25.00	22.00	8.00
Saucer	1.50	5.00	5.00	1.50
Sherbet, 6 oz	5.00	9.00	12.00	—
Soup bowl, flat, 7-3/4" d	10.00	—	—	16.00
Sugar	6.00	14.50	—	35.00
Tidbit, two tiers	—	—	35.00	—
Tumbler, 9 oz, water	6.00	—	16.00	—

Bubble, forest green sugar, **$14.50**.

Bubble, blue grill plate, **$22**; platter, **$18**; soup bowl, **$16**; berry bowl, 4" d, **$18**.

Cameo

Ballerina, Dancing Girl

Manufactured by Hocking Glass Company, Lancaster, Ohio, from 1930 to 1934.

Pieces are made in crystal, green, pink, and yellow. Only the crystal has a platinum rim.

Reproductions: † Salt shakers made in blue, green and pink. Children's dishes have been made in green and pink, but were never part of the original pattern. Recently, a squatty candy dish in cobalt blue has also been made, but this was not an original color.

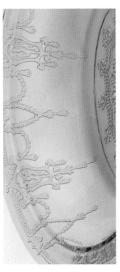

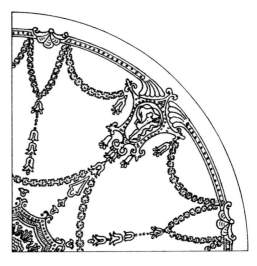

Item	Crystal	Green	Pink	Yellow
Berry bowl, 4-1/4" d	18.00	—	—	—
Berry bowl, 8-1/4" d	—	48.00	175.00	—
Butter dish, cov	—	250.00	—	1,500.00
Cake plate, 10" d, three legs	—	50.00	—	—
Cake plate, 10-1/2" d, flat	—	120.00	165.00	—
Candlesticks, pr, 4" h	—	150.00	—	—
Candy jar, cov, 4" h	—	110.00	495.00	125.00
Candy jar, cov, 6-1/2" h	—	195.00	—	—
Cereal bowl, 5-1/2" d	9.50	45.00	160.00	35.00
Champagne	—	45.00	—	—
Cocktail shaker	600.00	—	—	—
Comport, 5" w	—	65.00	200.00	—
Console bowl, three legs, 11" d	—	90.00	45.00	125.00
Cookie jar, cov	—	85.00	—	—
Cream soup bowl, 4-3/4" d	—	215.00	—	—
Creamer, 3-1/4" h	—	30.00	110.00	25.00
Creamer, 4-1/4" h	—	30.00	115.00	—
Cup	10.00	20.00	85.00	10.00
Decanter, 10" h	235.00	225.00	—	—
Domino tray, 7" l	165.00	275.00	265.00	—
Goblet, 6" h, water	—	95.00	195.00	—
Ice bowl, 3" h, 5-1/2" d	265.00	300.00	750.00	—
Jam jar, cov, 2" h	185.00	275.00	—	—
Juice pitcher, 6" h, 36 oz	—	110.00	—	—
Juice tumbler, 3 oz, ftd	—	65.00	90.00	—
Juice tumbler, 5 oz, 3-3/4" h	—	60.00	—	—
Mayonnaise, ftd	—	60.00	—	—
Pitcher, 8-1/2" h, 56 oz	550.00	70.00	1,450.00	—
Plate, 6" d, sherbet	6.00	12.50	90.00	4.00
Plate, 7" d, salad	12.00	13.50	—	—
Plate, 8" d, luncheon	8.00	18.00	36.00	12.50
Plate, 8-1/2", luncheon, sq	—	70.00	—	250.00
Plate, 9-1/2" d, dinner	—	30.00	85.00	15.00
Plate, 10-1/2" d, dinner, rimmed	—	115.00	175.00	—
Plate, 10-1/2" d, grill	—	20.00	55.00	14.50
Platter, 12" l	—	35.00	—	42.00
Relish, 7-1/2" l, ftd, three parts	175.00	40.00	—	—
Salad bowl, 7-1/4" d	—	70.00	—	—
Salt and pepper shakers, pr, ftd †	—	95.00	90.00	—
Sandwich plate, 10" d	—	30.00	45.00	—
Saucer	4.00	4.00	90.00	4.50
Sherbet, 3-1/8" h, blown	—	18.00	75.00	—
Sherbet, 3-1/8" h, molded	—	18.00	75.00	40.00
Sherbet, 4-7/8" h	—	40.00	100.00	45.00
Soup bowl, rimmed, 9" d	—	100.00	135.00	85.00
Sugar, 3-1/4" h	—	25.00	—	22.00

Item	Crystal	Green	Pink	Yellow
Sugar, 4-1/4" h	—	32.50	125.00	—
Syrup pitcher, 20 oz, 5-3/4" h	—	250.00	—	2,000.00
Tumbler, 9 oz, 4" h	16.00	32.00	80.00	—
Tumbler, 9 oz, 5" h, ftd	—	30.00	115.00	22.00
Tumbler, 10 oz, 4-3/4" h, flat	—	35.00	95.00	—
Tumbler, 11" oz, 5" h, flat	—	30.00	90.00	60.00
Tumbler, 11 oz, 5-3/4" h, ftd	—	75.00	135.00	—
Tumbler, 15 oz, 5-1/4" h	—	80.00	145.00	—
Tumbler, 15 oz, 6-3/8" h, ftd	—	495.00	—	—
Vase, 5-3/4" h	—	375.00	—	—
Vase, 8" h	—	75.00	—	—
Vegetable, oval, 10" l	—	55.00	—	48.00
Vinegar bottle	—	55.00	—	—
Wine, 3-1/2" h	—	1,200.00	950.00	—
Wine, 4" h	—	95.00	250.00	—

Cameo, green vegetable bowl, **$50.**

Cameo, crystal tumbler with platinum trim, **$16.**

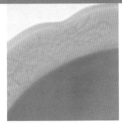

Cherry Blossom

Manufactured by Jeannette Glass Company, Jeannette, Pa., from 1930 to 1939.

Pieces are made in crystal, Delphite, green, jadeite, pink, and red (production was very limited in crystal, jadeite and red).

Reproductions: † Reproductions include a small berry bowl, an 8-1/2-inch diameter bowl, a covered butter dish, a cake plate, a cereal bowl, cup, pitcher, 6-inch and 9-inch plates, divided 13-inch platter, salt shaker, sandwich tray, saucer, and 3-3/4-inch and 4-1/2-inch-high footed tumblers. A child-size/toy saucer, creamer, and sugar have also been produced, as well as a children's butter dish, which was never included in original production. Reproductions have been made in cobalt blue, Delphite, green, pink, and red.

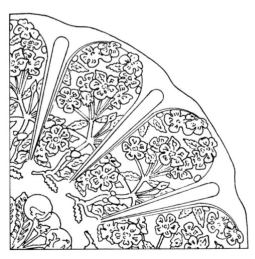

Item	Delphite	Green	Pink
Berry bowl, 4-3/4" d †	24.00	27.50	25.00
Berry bowl, 8-1/2" d †	45.00	55.00	50.00
Bowl, 9" d, two handles	27.50	95.00	48.00
Butter dish, cov †	—	115.00	75.00
Cake plate, 10-1/4" d, three legs †	—	38.00	35.00
Cereal bowl, 5-3/4" d †	—	35.00	60.00
Coaster		15.00	15.00
Creamer	30.00	20.00	25.00
Cup †	28.00	28.00	30.00
Fruit bowl, 10-1/2" d	32.00	120.00	135.00
Iced tea tumbler, PAT, flat	—	—	135.00
Juice tumbler, 1 oz, 3-1/2"	25.00	35.00	25.00
Mug, 7 oz	—	195.00	265.00
Pitcher, 36 oz, 6-3/4" h, 36 oz †	95.00	60.00	78.00
Pitcher, 36 oz, 8", PAT, ftd	—	65.00	75.00
Pitcher, 42 oz, 8", PAT, flat	—	65.00	95.00
Plate, 6" d, sherbet †	12.50	10.00	12.00
Plate, 7" d, salad	—	30.00	28.00
Plate, 9" d, dinner †	20.00	24.00	30.00
Plate, 9" d, grill	—	35.00	32.50
Plate, 10" d, grill	—	32.50	—
Platter, 11" l, oval	40.00	55.00	50.00
Platter, 13" d	—	150.00	150.00
Platter, 13" divided †	—	72.00	75.00
Salt and pepper shakers, pr, scalloped base †	—	995.00	1,250.00
Sandwich tray, 10-1/2" d †	20.00	30.00	45.00
Saucer †	6.00	8.00	6.50
Sherbet	24.00	30.00	22.00
Soup, flat, 7-3/4" d	—	90.00	80.00
Sugar, cov	20.00	27.50	35.00
Tray, 10-1/2" w handles	—	—	35.00
Tumbler, 3-3/4" h, AOP, ftd †	—	22.00	24.00
Tumbler, 5" h	20.00	70.00	72.00
Tumbler, 8 oz, 4-1/2" h, scalloped ftd base, AOP	—	40.00	42.00
Tumbler, 9 oz, 4-1/4" h	—	24.00	20.00
Tumbler, 9 oz, 4-1/2" h †	30.00	30.00	30.00
Vegetable bowl, 9" l, oval	45.00	42.00	40.00

Children's

Item	Delphite	Pink
Creamer	50.00	50.00
Cup †	42.00	65.00
Plate, 6" d	15.00	15.00
Saucer	7.50	7.50
Sugar	50.00	50.00

Cherry Blossom, Delphite berry bowls, 4-3/4" d, each **$17.50.**

Circle

Manufactured by Hocking Glass Company, Lancaster, Ohio, in the 1930s.

Pieces are made in crystal, green, and pink. Crystal is listed in the original catalogs, but few pieces have surfaced to date. A 3-1/8-inch diameter sherbet is known and valued at $4.

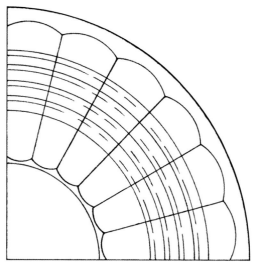

Item	Green	Pink
Bowl, 4-1/2" d	15.00	15.00
Bowl, 5-1/2" d, flared	17.50	17.50
Bowl, 8" d	16.00	16.00
Bowl, 9-3/8" d	18.50	18.50
Creamer, ftd	9.00	16.00
Cup	6.50	7.50
Goblet, 8 oz, 5-3/4" h	16.50	15.00
Iced tea tumbler, 10 oz	17.50	17.50
Juice tumbler, 4 oz	9.50	9.00
Pitcher, 60 oz	35.00	35.00
Pitcher, 80 oz	30.00	32.00
Plate, 6" d, sherbet	6.00	6.00
Plate, 8-1/4"d, luncheon	12.00	12.00
Plate, 9-1/2" d, dinner	12.00	12.00
Sandwich plate, 10" d	15.00	17.50
Saucer, 6" d	2.50	2.50
Sherbet, 3-1/8"	8.00	8.00
Sherbet, 4-3/4"	10.00	12.00
Sugar, ftd	12.00	16.00
Tumbler, 8 oz	10.00	10.00
Tumbler, 15 oz, flat	17.50	17.50
Wine, 4-1/2" h	15.00	15.00

Circle, green cup, **$6.**

Circle, green footed creamer, **$9**; green tumbler, flat, 15 oz, **$17.50.**

Circle, from left: green tumbler, 8 oz, **$10**; green sherbet, 4-3/4" h, **$10;** green sherbet, 3-1/8" h, **$8.**

Circle, items have frosted green stems and clear tops; from left: wine, 4-1/2" h, **$15**; sherbet, 4-3/4" h, **$10;** sherbet, 3-1/8" h, **$8.**

Circle, green pitcher, 80 oz, **$30.** A reamer is known that fits on top of the pitcher. A 60-oz pitcher is also known and rare.

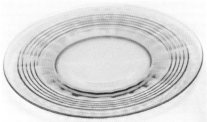

Circle, green berry bowl, 5", **$17.50**; green bowl, **$15,** on a sherbet plate, **$6**; associated ladle, **$10.**

Circle, green luncheon plate, 8-1/4", **$12**; green flared cup, **$6.50,** on a 6" saucer, **$2.50.** Two styles of cups are known: flared sides and round sides.

Cloverleaf

Manufactured by Hazel Atlas Glass Company, Clarksburg, W.V., and Zanesville, Ohio, from 1930 to 1936.

Pieces are made in black, crystal, green, pink, and yellow. Collector interest in crystal is minimal; prices would be about 50 percent of those listed for green.

Item	Black	Green	Pink	Yellow
Ashtray, match holder in center, 4" d	65.00	—	—	—
Ashtray, match holder in center, 5-3/4" d	90.00	—	—	—
Bowl, 8" d	—	95.00	—	—
Candy dish, cov	—	65.00	—	130.00
Cereal bowl, 5" d	—	50.00	—	55.00
Creamer, 3-5/8" h, ftd	25.00	12.00	—	24.00
Cup	20.00	12.00	8.00	12.00
Dessert bowl, 4" d	—	30.00	30.00	35.00
Plate, 6" d, sherbet	40.00	6.50	—	10.00
Plate, 8" d, luncheon	18.00	15.00	12.00	18.00
Plate, 10-1/4" d, grill	—	25.00	—	40.00
Salad bowl, 7" d	—	60.00	—	65.00
Salt and pepper shakers, pr	100.00	40.00	—	140.00
Saucer	10.00	10.00	7.00	5.00
Sherbet, 3" h, ftd	22.00	25.00	10.00	16.00
Sugar, 3-5/8" h, ftd	25.00	12.00	—	24.00
Tumbler, 9 oz, 4" h, flat	—	65.00	26.50	35.00
Tumbler, 10 oz, 3-3/4" h, flat	—	50.00	30.00	—
Tumbler, 10 oz, 5-3/4" h, ftd	—	50.00	—	40.00

Cloverleaf, green saucer, **$10**; pink plate, **$12**; pink cup, **$8**.

Colonial

Knife and Fork

Manufactured by Hocking Glass Company, Lancaster, Ohio, from 1934 to 1938.

Pieces are made in crystal, green, and pink.

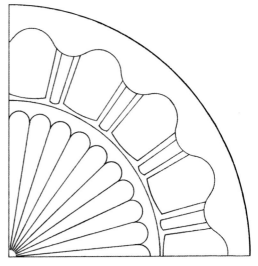

Item	Crystal	Green	Pink
Berry bowl, 3-3/4" d	—	—	60.00
Berry bowl, 4-1/2"	10.00	20.00	18.00
Berry bowl, 9" d	24.00	36.00	35.00
Butter dish, cov	45.00	60.00	700.00
Cereal bowl, 5-1/2" d	32.00	85.00	60.00
Claret, 4 oz, 5-1/4" h	21.00	31.50	—
Cocktail, 3 oz, 4" h	15.00	27.50	—
Cordial, 1 oz, 3-3/4" h	25.00	30.00	—
Cream soup bowl, 4-1/2" d	70.00	85.00	72.00
Creamer, 8 oz, 5" h	20.00	25.00	65.00
Cup	8.00	15.00	12.00
Goblet, 8-1/2 oz, 5-3/4" h	20.00	36.00	40.00
Iced tea tumbler, 12 oz	28.00	55.00	45.00
Juice tumbler, 5 oz, 3" h	17.50	27.50	24.50
Lemonade tumbler, 15 oz	47.50	75.00	65.00
Milk pitcher, 8 oz, 5" h	25.00	25.00	65.00
Mug, 12 oz, 5-1/2" h	—	825.00	500.00
Pitcher, 54 oz, 7" h, ice lip	40.00	45.00	48.00
Pitcher, 54 oz, 7" h, no lip	40.00	45.00	48.00
Pitcher, 68 oz, 7-3/4" h, ice lip	35.00	72.00	65.00
Pitcher, 68 oz, 7-3/4" h, no lip	45.00	72.00	65.00
Plate, 6" d, sherbet	4.50	10.00	7.00
Plate, 8-1/2" d, luncheon	6.00	8.00	10.00
Plate, 10" d, dinner	35.00	67.50	65.00
Plate, 10"d, grill	17.50	30.00	27.50
Plate, 12" d, oval	17.50	25.00	30.00
Platter, 12" l, oval	17.50	25.00	35.00
Salt and pepper shakers, pr	60.00	160.00	150.00
Saucer	4.50	7.50	6.50
Sherbet, 3" h	—	—	24.00
Sherbet, 3-3/8" h	10.00	18.00	12.00
Soup bowl, 7" d	30.00	85.00	85.00
Spoon holder or celery vase	105.00	130.00	135.00
Sugar, cov	90.00	55.00	50.00
Sugar, 5", open	10.00	12.00	15.00
Tumbler, 3 oz, 3-1/4" h, ftd	18.00	20.00	16.00
Tumbler, 5 oz, 4" h, ftd	15.00	35.00	24.50
Tumbler, 9 oz, 4" h	15.00	20.00	25.00
Tumbler, 10 oz, 5-1/4" h, ftd	30.00	48.50	50.00
Tumbler, 11 oz, 5-1/8" h	25.00	37.50	45.00
Vegetable bowl, 10" l, oval	18.00	25.00	30.00
Whiskey, 2-1/2" h, 1-1/2 oz	9.00	20.00	18.00
Wine, 4-1/2" h, 2-1/2 oz	18.00	30.00	15.00

Colonial, green saucer, **$7.50.**

Colonial, green creamer, **$25**; sugar, **$12.**

Colonial, crystal wine, **$18**; cocktail, **$15.**

Colonial Block

Manufactured by Hazel Atlas Glass Company, Clarksburg, W.V., and Zanesville, Ohio, early 1930s.

Pieces are made in black, cobalt blue (rare), crystal, green, pink, and white (1950s).

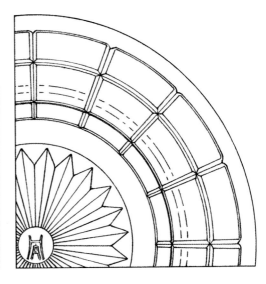

Item	Black	Crystal	Green	Pink	White
Bowl, 4" d	—	6.00	10.00	10.00	—
Bowl, 7" d	—	16.00	35.00	20.00	—
Butter dish, cov	—	35.00	50.00	45.00	—
Butter tub, cov	—	35.00	40.00	40.00	—
Candy jar, cov	—	30.00	45.00	40.00	—
Compote, 4" h, 4-3/4" w	—	12.00	—	—	—
Creamer	—	15.00	16.00	15.00	7.50
Goblet, 5-3/4" h	—	9.00	12.00	15.00	—
Pitcher, 20 oz, 5-3/4" h	—	40.00	50.00	50.00	—
Powder jar, cov	30.00	20.00	24.00	24.00	—
Sherbet	—	6.00	10.00	9.50	—
Sugar, cov	—	20.00	25.00	25.00	20.00
Sugar, open	—	10.00	8.00	8.00	10.00

Colonial Block, green covered butter dish, **$50.**

Colonial Fluted
Rope

Manufactured by Federal Glass Company, Columbus, Ohio, from 1928 to 1933.

Pieces are made in crystal and green.

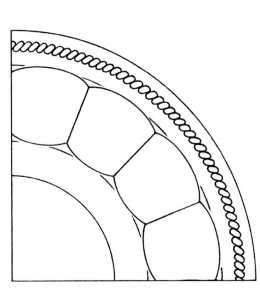

Item	Crystal	Green
Berry bowl, 4" d	11.00	12.00
Berry bowl, 7-1/2" d	16.00	30.00
Cereal bowl, 6" d	15.00	18.00
Creamer, ftd	12.00	14.00
Cup	5.00	7.50
Plate, 6" d, sherbet	2.50	4.50
Plate, 8" d, luncheon	5.00	10.00
Salad bowl, 6-1/2" d, 2-1/2" deep	22.00	35.00
Saucer	2.50	4.00
Sherbet	6.00	8.50
Sugar, cov	21.00	25.00
Sugar, open	8.00	10.00

Colonial Fluted, green sugar, **$10.**

Colonial Fluted, green creamer, **$14.**

Columbia

Manufactured by Federal Glass Company, Columbus, Ohio, from 1938 to 1942.

Pieces are made in crystal and pink. Several flashed (stained) colors are found, and some decaled pieces are known.

Reproductions: † The 2-7/8-inch high juice tumbler has been reproduced. Look for the "France" on the base to clearly identify the reproductions.

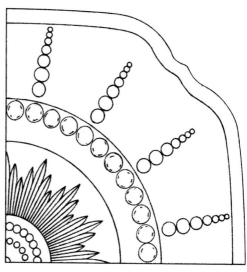

Item	Crystal	Flashed	Pink
Bowl, 8-1/2" d	20.00	—	—
Bowl, 10-1/2" d, ruffled edge	20.00	20.00	—
Butter dish, cov	22.00	25.00	—
Cereal bowl, 5" d	18.50	—	—
Chop plate, 11" d	17.00	12.00	—
Crescent shaped salad	27.00	—	—
Cup	8.50	10.00	25.00
Juice tumbler, 4 oz, 2-3/4" h †	30.00	—	—
Lamp shade, 8-1/2" d	25.00	—	—
Plate, 6" d, bread and butter	5.00	4.00	14.00
Plate, 9-1/2" d, luncheon	15.00	12.00	32.00
Salad bowl, 8-1/2" d	20.00	—	—
Saucer	4.50	4.00	10.00
Snack tray, cup	30.00	—	—
Soup bowl, 8" d, low	25.00	—	—
Tumbler, 9 oz	32.50	—	—

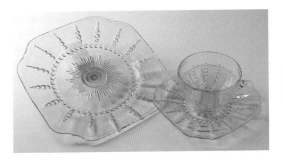

Columbia, crystal luncheon plate **$15**; cup, **$8.50**; saucer, **$4.50**.

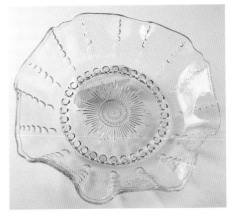

Columbia, crystal ruffled bowl, **$20**.

Constellation
Pattern #300

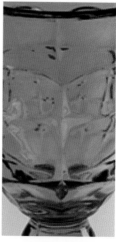

Manufactured by Indiana Glass Company, Dunkirk, Ind., c1940. Later reissued as Sunset Constellation by Tiara Home products in the 1980s.

Pieces are made in crystal and amber by Indiana. Made in amberina, emerald green, red, and yellow mist by Tiara.

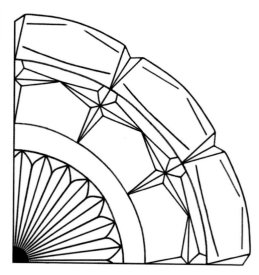

Item	Amber	Crystal	Tiara Colors
Basket, 11"	—	30.00	25.00
Bowl, 11" d, two handles	—	25.00	12.00
Buffet plate, 18" d	—	40.00	—
Cake stand	—	50.00	—
Candlesticks, pr	—	45.00	15.00
Candy dish, cov	—	25.00	18.00
Celery tray	—	20.00	—
Console bowl, 11-1/2" d	—	25.00	20.00
Cookie jar, cov	—	28.00	24.00
Creamer	—	10.00	—
Goblet, water	15.00	15.00	12.00
Mayonnaise bowl, ladle, underplate	—	28.00	—
Mug	—	15.00	—
Nappy, three toes	—	15.00	—
Nut bowl, 6" d, cupped	—	12.00	—
Pickle, oval	—	15.00	—
Pitcher, 7-1/2" d	65.00	45.00	60.00
Plate, dessert	—	5.00	—
Plate, lunch	—	8.00	—
Plate, salad	—	10.00	—
Platter, oval	—	20.00	—
Punch bowl	—	35.00	—
Relish, three parts	—	15.00	—
Salad bowl	—	22.00	—
Serving plate, 13-1/2" d	—	25.00	15.00
Sugar	—	10.00	—
Tumbler, 8 oz	—	15.00	—

Constellation, amber water goblet, **$15.**

Constellation, crystal nut bowl, **$12.**

Coronation
Banded Fine Rib, Saxon

Manufactured by Hocking Glass Company, Lancaster, Ohio, from 1936 to 1940.

Pieces are made in crystal, green, pink, and Royal Ruby.

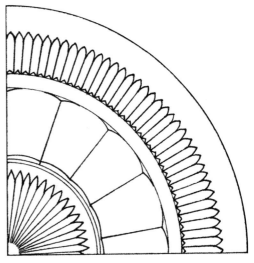

Item	Crystal	Green	Pink	Royal Ruby
Berry bowl, 4-1/4" d	—	50.00	9.00	9.50
Berry bowl, 8" d, handles	—	—	18.00	20.00
Berry bowl, 8" d	—	195.00	—	—
Cup	5.00	—	6.00	7.50
Nappy bowl, 6-1/2" d	15.00	—	7.50	15.00
Pitcher, 68 oz, 7-3/4" h	—	—	500.00	—
Plate, 6" d, sherbet	2.00	—	5.00	
Plate, 8-1/2" d, luncheon	5.00	60.00	15.00	8.50
Saucer	2.00	—	5.00	
Sherbet	—	85.00	7.00	—
Tumbler, 10 oz, 5" h, ftd	—	195.00	35.00	—

Coronation, royal ruby handled berry bowl, **$20.**

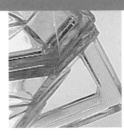

Cracked Ice

Manufactured by Indiana Glass, Dunkirk, Ind., in the 1930s.

Pieces are made in pink and green. This pattern is often mistaken for Tea Room, so look for the additional diagonal line, giving it a more Art Deco style.

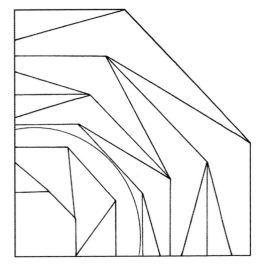

Item	Green	Pink
Creamer	30.00	35.00
Plate, 6-1/2" d	15.00	18.00
Sherbet	12.00	15.00
Sugar, cov	30.00	35.00
Tumbler	30.00	32.50

Cracked Ice, pink creamer, **$35.**

Cracked Ice, pink covered sugar, **$35.**

Cube
Cubist

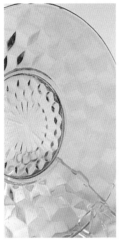

Manufactured by Jeannette Glass Company, Jeannette, Pa., from 1929 to 1933.

Pieces are made in amber, crystal, green, pink, ultramarine, and white. Production in amber and white is limited to the 2-3/8-inch high sugar bowl, and is valued at $3.

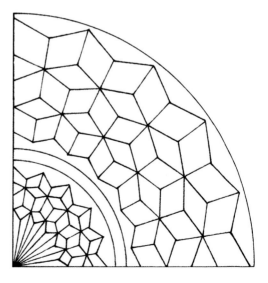

Item	Crystal	Green	Pink	Ultramarine
Bowl, 4-1/2" d, deep	—	7.00	10.00	35.00
Butter dish, cov	—	95.00	100.00	—
Candy jar, cov, 6-1/2" h	—	55.00	40.00	—
Coaster, 3-1/4" d	—	10.00	10.00	—
Creamer, 2-5/8" h	5.00	10.00	12.00	70.00
Creamer, 3-9/16" h	—	9.00	9.00	—
Cup	—	7.00	8.00	—
Dessert bowl, 4-1/2" d, pointed rim	4.00	8.50	9.50	—
Pitcher, 8-3/4" h, 45 oz	—	265.00	215.00	—
Plate, 6" d, sherbet	—	11.00	3.50	—
Plate, 8" d, luncheon	—	8.50	7.50	—
Powder jar, cov, three legs	—	30.00	30.00	—
Salad bowl, 6-1/2" d	6.00	15.00	15.00	—
Salt and pepper shakers, pr	—	40.00	36.00	—
Saucer	1.50	3.00	4.50	—
Sherbet, ftd	—	8.50	12.00	—
Sugar, cov, 2-3/8" h	4.00	24.00	6.00	—
Sugar, cov, 3" h	—	35.00	25.00	—
Sugar, open, 3"	5.00	8.00	7.00	—
Tray, 7-1/2" l	8.50	—	5.00	—
Tumbler, 9 oz, 4" h	—	70.00	65.00	—

Cube, pink luncheon plate, **$7.50.**

Daisy

No. 620

Manufactured by Indiana Glass Company, Dunkirk, Ind., from late 1930s to 1980s.

Pieces are made in amber (1940s), crystal (1933-40), dark green (1960s-80s), fired-on red (late 1930s), and milk glass (1960s-80s).

Item	Amber or Fired-On Red	Crystal or Milk White	Dark Green
Berry bowl, 4-1/2" d	12.00	6.00	6.00
Berry bowl, 7-3/8" d	15.50	8.50	12.50
Berry bowl, 9-3/8" d	35.00	26.00	14.00
Cake plate, 11-1/2" d	16.50	12.00	14.00
Cereal bowl, 6" d	25.00	10.00	10.00
Cream soup bowl, 4-1/2" d	12.50	7.50	12.50
Creamer, ftd	10.00	8.00	5.00
Cup	6.00	4.00	6.00
Plate, 6" d, sherbet	3.00	4.50	5.00
Plate, 7-3/8" d, salad	8.50	8.50	9.00
Plate, 8-3/8" d, luncheon	6.00	10.00	12.00
Plate, 9-3/8" d, dinner	9.00	12.00	10.00
Plate, 10-3/8" d, grill	15.00	5.50	18.00
Plate, 10-3/8" d, grill, indent for soup	15.00	8.00	8.00
Platter, 10-3/4" d	16.00	11.00	15.00
Relish dish, 8-3/8" d, three parts	24.00	12.00	12.00
Sandwich plate, 11-1/2" d	16.50	6.00	14.00
Saucer	5.00	6.00	5.00
Sherbet, ftd	10.00	5.00	10.00
Sugar, ftd	10.00	8.00	10.00
Tumbler, 9 oz, ftd	16.00	10.00	10.00
Tumbler, 12 oz, ftd	40.00	15.00	22.00
Vegetable bowl, 10" l, oval	20.00	18.00	18.00

Daisy, amber creamer, **$10.**

Daisy, green luncheon plate, **$12.**

Daisy, amber luncheon plate, **$6.**

Daisy, crystal luncheon plate, **$10.**

Dewdrop

Manufactured by Jeannette Glass Company, Jeannette, Pa., from 1953 to 1956.

Pieces are made in crystal.

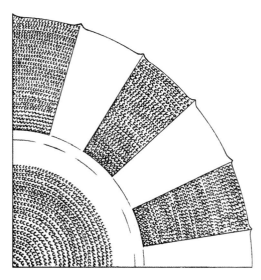

Item	Crystal
Bowl, 4-3/4" d	9.00
Bowl, 8-1/2" d	22.00
Bowl, 10-3/8" d	24.00
Butter, cov	32.00
Candy dish, cov, 7" d	30.00
Casserole, cov	27.50
Creamer	8.50
Cup	4.00
Iced tea tumbler, 15 oz	17.50
Lazy Susan, 13" d tray	30.00
Pitcher, 1/2 gallon, ftd	48.00

Item	Crystal
Plate, 11-1/2" d	20.00
Punch cup	4.00
Punch bowl set, bowl, 12 cups	90.00
Snack cup	4.00
Snack plate, indent for cup	8.00
Relish, leaf-shape, handle	9.00
Sugar, cov	14.00
Tray, 10" d	22.00
Tumbler, 9 oz	15.00

Dewdrop, crystal sugar, **$8.50**; creamer, **$8.50.**

Dewdrop, crystal tumbler, **$15**; iridescent pitcher, **$48.**

Diamond Quilted
Flat Diamond

Manufactured by Imperial Glass Company, Bellaire, Ohio, from late 1920 to early 1930s.

Pieces are made in amber, black, blue, crystal, green, pink, and red. Amber and red prices would be valued slightly higher than black.

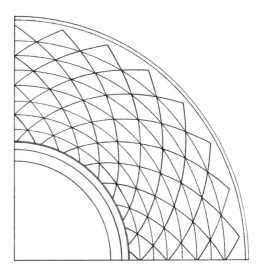

Item	Black	Blue	Crystal
Bowl, 5-1/2" d, one handle	20.00	—	—
Bowl, 7" d, crimped edge	22.00	—	—
Cake salver, 10" d, tall	—	—	—
Candlesticks, pr	60.00	—	50.00
Candy jar, cov, ftd	—	—	25.00
Cereal bowl, 5" d	15.00	—	8.00
Champagne, 9 oz, 6" h	—	—	—
Compote, 6" h, 7-1/4" w	—	—	—
Compote, cov, 11-1/2" d	—	—	—
Console bowl, 10-1/2" d, rolled edge	65.00	60.00	15.00
Cordial, 1 oz	—	—	—
Cream soup bowl, 4-3/4" d	22.00	20.00	20.00
Creamer	18.50	20.00	15.00
Cup	18.00	18.50	7.00
Ice bucket	90.00	90.00	—
Iced tea tumbler, 12 oz	—	—	—
Mayonnaise set, comport, plate, ladle	60.00	65.00	25.00
Pitcher, 64 oz	—	—	—
Plate, 6" d, sherbet	10.00	9.00	7.50
Plate, 7" d, salad	10.00	10.00	8.00
Plate, 8" d, luncheon	12.00	16.00	9.00
Punch bowl and stand	—	—	—
Sandwich plate, 14" d	—	—	—
Sandwich server, center handle	50.00	50.00	20.00
Saucer	5.00	5.00	2.00
Sherbet	16.00	16.00	14.00
Sugar	20.00	25.00	12.00
Tumbler, 6 oz, ftd	—	—	—
Tumbler, 9 oz	—	—	—
Tumbler, 9 oz, ftd	—	—	—
Tumbler, 12 oz, ftd	—	—	—
Vase, fan	80.00	75.00	—
Whiskey, 1-1/2" oz	—	—	—
Wine, 2 oz	—	—	—
Wine, 3 oz	—	—	—

Additional colors

Item	Green	Pink
Bowl, 5-1/2" d, one handle	15.00	18.00
Bowl, 7" d, crimped edge	20.00	25.00
Cake salver, 10" d, tall	60.00	65.00
Candlesticks, pr	30.00	28.00
Candy jar, cov, ftd	65.00	65.00
Cereal bowl, 5" d	9.00	8.50
Champagne, 9 oz, 6" h	12.00	—
Compote, 6" h, 7-1/4" w	45.00	48.00
Compote, cov, 11-1/2" d	80.00	75.00
Console bowl, 10-1/2" d, rolled edge	20.00	40.00
Cordial, 1 oz	12.00	15.00
Cream soup bowl, 4-3/4" d	20.00	14.00
Creamer	12.00	14.00
Cup	10.00	12.00
Ice bucket	50.00	50.00
Iced tea tumbler, 12 oz	10.00	10.00
Mayonnaise set, comport, plate, ladle	37.50	40.00
Pitcher, 64 oz	50.00	55.00
Plate, 6" d, sherbet	7.00	7.50
Plate, 7" d, salad	8.50	8.50
Plate, 8" d, luncheon	6.50	8.50
Punch bowl and stand	450.00	450.00
Sandwich plate, 14" d	15.00	15.00
Sandwich server, center handle	25.00	25.00
Saucer	4.00	4.00
Sherbet	10.00	10.00
Sugar	12.50	12.00
Tumbler, 6 oz, ftd	9.00	10.00
Tumbler, 9 oz	14.00	16.00
Tumbler, 9 oz, ftd	14.00	16.00
Tumbler, 12 oz, ftd	15.00	15.00
Vase, fan	50.00	50.00
Whiskey, 1-1/2" oz	10.00	12.00
Wine, 2 oz	12.50	12.50
Wine, 3 oz	15.00	15.00

Diamond Quilted, pink sugar, **$12.**

Diamond Quilted, pink creamer, **$14.**

Diana

Manufactured by Federal Glass Company, Columbus, Ohio, from 1937 to 1941.

Made in amber, crystal, and pink.

Reproductions: † A 13-1/8-inch diameter scalloped pink bowl has been made, which was not original to the pattern.

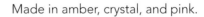

Diana, crystal tumbler, **$18.**   Diana, pink sherbet, **$12.**

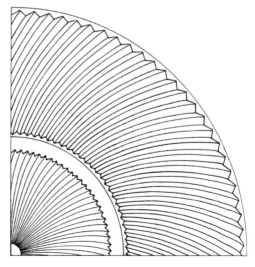

Item	Amber	Crystal	Pink
Ashtray, 3-1/2" d	—	4.00	5.00
Bowl, 12" d, scalloped edge	20.00	15.00	32.50
Candy jar, cov, round	40.00	18.50	48.00
Cereal bowl, 5" d	15.00	6.50	15.00
Coaster, 3-1/2" d	12.00	4.00	8.00
Console/fruit bowl, 11" d	12.00	20.00	44.00
Cream soup bowl, 5-1/2" d	18.00	14.00	24.00
Creamer, oval	12.00	5.00	12.50
Cup	7.00	4.00	19.00
Demitasse cup and saucer, 2 oz, 4-1/2" d saucer	—	12.50	45.00
Junior set, six cups and saucers, rack	—	125.00	300.00
Plate, 6" d, bread and butter	3.50	2.00	9.50
Plate, 9-1/2" d, dinner	9.00	6.00	18.50
Platter, 12" l, oval	16.50	12.00	28.00
Salad bowl, 9" d	18.00	15.00	30.00
Salt and pepper shakers, pr	100.00	30.00	75.00
Sandwich plate, 11-3/4" d	15.00	9.50	28.00
Sandwich plate, 11-3/4" d, advertising in center	—	15.00	—
Saucer	2.25	2.00	5.00
Sherbet	12.00	7.00	12.00
Sugar, open, oval	12.00	10.00	16.00
Tumbler, 9 oz, 4-1/8" h	30.00	18.00	45.00

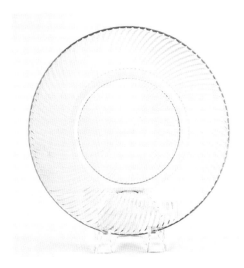

Diana, pink dinner plate, **$18.50.**

Dogwood
Apple Blossom, Wild Rose

Manufactured by Macbeth-Evans Company, Charleroi, Pa., from 1929 to 1932.

Made in Cremax, crystal, green, Monax, pink and yellow. Yellow is rare; a cereal bowl is known and valued at $95. Crystal items are valued at 50 percent less than green.

Item	Cremax or Monax	Green	Pink
Berry bowl, 8-1/2" d	40.00	100.00	65.00
Cake plate, 11" d, heavy solid foot	—	—	650.00
Cake plate, 13" d, heavy solid foot	185.00	135.00	165.00
Cereal bowl, 5-1/2" d	12.00	35.00	35.00
Coaster, 3-1/4" d	—	—	450.00
Creamer, 2-1/2" h, thin	—	48.00	35.00
Creamer, 3-1/4" h, thick	—	—	25.00
Cup, thin	—	32.00	20.00
Cup, thick	36.00	40.00	20.00
Fruit bowl, 10-1/4" d	100.00	250.00	550.00
Pitcher, 8" h, 80 oz, (American Sweetheart style)	—	—	1,250.00
Pitcher, 8" h, 80 oz, decorated	—	550.00	295.00
Plate, 6" d, bread and butter	25.00	10.00	10.00
Plate, 8" d, luncheon	—	12.00	12.00
Plate, 9-1/4" d, dinner	—	—	45.00
Plates, 10-1/2" d, grill, AOP or border design only	—	24.00	35.00
Platter, 12" d, oval	—	—	725.00
Salver, 12" d	175.00	—	45.00
Saucer	20.00	10.00	8.00
Sherbet, low, ftd	—	95.00	42.00
Sugar, 2-1/2" h, thin	—	50.00	30.00
Sugar, 3-1/4" h, thick, ftd	—	—	20.00
Tidbit, 2 tier	—	—	90.00
Tumbler, 10 oz, 4" h, decorated	—	100.00	55.00
Tumbler, 11 oz, 4-3/4" h, decorated	—	95.00	125.00
Tumbler, 12 oz, 5" h, decorated	—	125.00	75.00
Tumbler, molded band	—	—	25.00

Dogwood, pink sugar, **$20**; creamer, **$25**; luncheon plate, **$12.**

Doric

Manufactured by Jeannette Glass Company, Jeannette, Pa., from 1935 to 1938.

Pieces are made in Delphite, green, pink, and yellow. Yellow is rare.

Item	Delphite	Green	Pink
Berry bowl, 4-1/2" d	50.00	10.00	12.00
Berry bowl, 8-1/4" d	150.00	38.00	35.00
Bowl, 9" d, two handles	—	45.00	45.00
Butter dish, cov	—	90.00	75.00
Cake plate, 10" d, three legs	—	30.00	30.00
Candy dish, cov, 8" d	—	42.50	45.00
Candy dish, three parts	12.00	20.00	14.50
Cereal bowl, 5-1/2" d	—	65.00	95.00
Coaster, 3" d	—	28.00	20.00
Cream soup, 5" d, two handles	—	385.00	—
Creamer, 4" h	—	17.00	14.00
Cup	—	10.00	10.00
Pitcher, 36 oz, 6" h, flat	1,200.00	75.00	45.00
Pitcher, 48 oz, 7-1/2" h, ftd	—	1,000.00	750.00
Plate, 6" d, sherbet	—	7.50	7.50
Plate, 7" d, salad	—	20.00	18.00
Plate, 9" d, dinner	—	24.00	20.00
Plate, 9" d, grill	—	20.00	30.00
Platter, 12" l, oval	—	32.00	35.00
Relish tray, 4" x 4"	—	12.00	16.00
Relish tray, 4" x 8"	—	20.00	17.50
Salt and pepper shakers, pr	—	40.00	45.00
Saucer	—	7.00	5.00
Sherbet, footed	12.00	17.50	15.00
Sugar, cov	—	35.00	32.00
Tray, 8" x 8", serving	—	30.00	42.50
Tray, 10" l, handle	—	25.00	20.00
Tumbler, 9 oz, 4-1/2" h, flat	—	100.00	75.00
Tumbler, 10 oz, 4" h, ftd.	—	90.00	85.00
Tumbler, 12 oz, 5" h, ftd.	—	125.00	85.00
Vegetable bowl, 9" l, oval	—	45.00	50.00

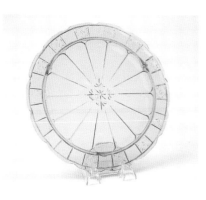

Doric, green cake plate, **$30.**

Doric and Pansy

Manufactured by Jeannette Glass Company, Jeannette, Pa., from 1937 to 1938.

Pieces are made in ultramarine, with limited production in pink and crystal.

Doric and Pansy, pink dinner plate, **$8.**

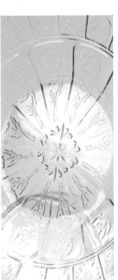

Item	Crystal	Pink	Ultramarine
Berry bowl, 4-1/2" d	12.00	12.00	25.00
Berry bowl, 8" d	—	24.00	75.00
Bowl, 9" d, handle	15.00	20.00	35.00
Butter dish, cov	—	—	600.00
Candy, cov, three parts	—	—	22.50
Cup	12.00	14.00	20.00
Creamer	72.00	90.00	145.00
Plate, 6" d, sherbet	8.00	12.00	22.00
Plate, 7" d, salad	—	—	40.00
Plate, 9" d, dinner	7.50	8.00	30.00
Salt shaker, orig top	—	—	325.00
Saucer	4.50	4.50	5.50
Sugar, open	80.00	85.00	145.00
Tray, 10" l, handles	45.00	—	35.00
Tumbler, 9 oz, 4-1/2" h	—	—	500.00

Children's

Item	Pink	Ultramarine
Creamer	42.00	50.00
Cup	35.00	48.00
Plate	12.00	12.50
Saucer	7.00	8.50
Sugar	35.00	50.00
14-pc set, orig box	400.00	425.00

Doric and Pansy, ultramarine child's sugar, **$50.**

Doric and Pansy, ultramarine child's creamer, **$50.**

English Hobnail
Line #555

Manufactured by Westmoreland Glass Company, Grapeville, Pa., from the 1920s to 1983.

Pieces are made in amber, cobalt blue, crystal, crystal with various color treatments, green, ice blue, pink, red, and turquoise blue. Values for cobalt blue, red or turquoise blue pieces would be about 25 percent higher than ice blue values. Currently, a turquoise basket is valued at $150; a red basket at $100. Crystal pieces with a color accent would be slightly higher than crystal values.

Reproductions: † A creamer and sugar with a hexagonal foot have been reproduced, as well as a nut bowl and pickle dish.

Item	Amber	Crystal	Green	Ice Blue	Pink
Ashtray, 3" d	20.00	20.00	24.00	—	24.00
Ashtray, 4-1/2" d	9.00	9.00	15.00	24.00	15.00
Ashtray, 4-1/2" sq	9.50	9.50	15.00	—	15.00
Basket, 5" d, handle	20.00	20.00	—	—	—
Basket, 6" d, handle, tall	40.00	40.00	—	—	43.00
Bonbon, 6-1/2" h, handle	15.00	17.50	30.00	40.00	30.00
Bowl, 7" d, six parts	17.50	17.50	—	—	—
Bowl, 7" d, oblong spoon	17.50	17.50	—	—	—
Bowl, 8" d, ftd	30.00	30.00	48.00	—	48.00
Bowl, 8" d, hexagonal foot, two handles	38.00	38.00	75.00	115.00	75.00
Bowl, 8", six pt	24.00	24.00	—	—	—
Bowl, 9-1/2" d, round, crimped	30.00	30.00	—	—	—
Bowl, 10" d, flared	35.00	35.00	40.00	—	40.00
Bowl, 10" l, oval, crimped	40.00	40.00	—	—	—
Bowl, 11" d, bell	35.00	35.00	—	—	—
Bowl, 11" d, rolled edge	35.00	35.00	40.00	85.00	40.00
Bowl, 12" d, flared	32.00	32.00	40.00	—	95.00
Bowl, 12" l, oval crimped	32.00	32.00	—	—	—
Candelabra, two lite	20.00	20.00	—	—	—
Candlesticks, pr, 3-1/2" h, round base	24.00	32.00	36.00	—	60.00
Candlesticks, pr, 5-1/2" h, sq base	30.00	32.00	—	—	—
Candlesticks, pr, 9" h, round base	50.00	40.00	72.00	—	125.00
Candy dish, three feet	45.00	38.00	50.00	—	50.00
Candy dish, cov, 1/2 lb, cone shape	45.00	40.00	55.00	—	90.00
Celery, 12" l, oval	24.00	45.00	36.00	—	36.00
Celery, 9" d	18.00	20.00	32.00	—	32.00
Champagne, two ball, round foot	8.00	7.00	20.00	—	20.00
Chandelier, 17" shade, 200 prisms	425.00	400.00	—	—	—
Cheese, cov, 6" d	40.00	42.00	—	—	—
Cheese, cov, 8-3/4" d	50.00	48.00	—	—	—
Cigarette box, cov, 4-1/2 x 2-1/2"	24.50	24.50	30.00	—	55.00
Cigarette jar, cov, round	16.00	18.00	25.00	—	65.00
Claret, 5 oz, round	15.00	17.50	—	—	—
Coaster, 3"	5.00	5.00	—	—	—
Cocktail, 3 oz, round	8.50	12.00	—	—	37.50

Item	Amber	Crystal	Green	Ice Blue	Pink
Cocktail, 3-1/2 oz, round, ball	15.00	17.50	—	—	—
Compote, 5" d, round, round foot	22.00	20.00	25.00	—	25.00
Compote, 5" d, round, sq foot	24.00	24.00	—	—	—
Compote, 5-1/2" d, bell	12.00	15.00	—	—	—
Compote, 5-1/2" d, bell, sq foot	20.00	20.00	—	—	—
Console bowl, 12" d, flange	30.00	30.00	40.00	—	40.00
Cordial, 1 oz, round, ball	16.50	17.50	—	—	—
Cordial, 1 oz, round, foot	16.50	16.50	—	—	—
Cream soup bowl, 4-5/8" d	15.00	15.00	—	—	—
Cream soup liner, round, 6-1/2" d	5.00	5.00	—	—	—
Creamer, hexagonal foot †	20.00	20.00	25.00	—	48.00
Creamer, low, flat	10.00	10.00	—	—	—
Creamer, sq foot	24.00	24.00	45.00	—	45.00
Cruet, 12 oz	—	25.00	—	—	—
Cup	8.00	12.00	18.00	—	25.00
Decanter, 20 oz	55.00	55.00	—	—	—
Demitasse cup	17.50	17.50	55.00	—	55.00
Dish, 6" d, crimped	15.00	15.00	—	—	—
Eggcup	15.00	15.00	—	—	—
Finger bowl, 4-1/2" d	7.50	7.50	15.00	35.00	15.00
Finger bowl, 4-1/2" sq, foot	9.50	9.50	18.00	40.00	18.00
Finger bowl liner, 6" sq	6.50	7.00	20.00	—	20.00
Finger bowl liner, 6-1/2" d, round	12.00	12.00	10.00	—	10.00
Ginger ale tumbler, 5 oz, flat	10.00	10.00	18.00	—	20.00
Ginger ale tumbler, 5 oz, round foot	10.00	10.00	—	—	—
Ginger ale tumbler, 5 oz, sq foot	8.00	8.00	32.00	—	35.00
Goblet, 8 oz, 6-1/4" h, round, water	12.00	12.00	—	50.00	35.00
Goblet, 8 oz, sq foot, water	10.00	10.00	—	—	50.00
Grapefruit bowl, 6-1/2" d	12.00	12.00	22.00	—	24.00
Hat, high	18.00	18.00	—	—	—
Hat, low	15.00	15.00	—	—	—
Honey compote, 6" d, round foot	18.00	18.00	35.00	—	35.00
Honey compote, 6" d, sq foot	18.00	18.00	—	—	—
Ice tub, 4" h	18.00	18.00	50.00	—	85.00
Ice tub, 5-1/2" h	36.00	36.00	65.00	—	100.00
Iced tea tumbler, 10 oz	14.00	14.00	30.00	—	30.00
Iced tea tumbler, 11 oz, round, ball	12.00	12.00	—	—	—

Item	Amber	Crystal	Green	Ice Blue	Pink
Iced tea tumbler, 11 oz, sq foot	13.50	13.50	—	—	—
Iced tea tumbler, 12-1/2 oz, round foot	14.00	24.00	—	—	—
Iced tea tumbler, 12 oz, flat	14.00	14.00	32.00	—	32.00
Icer, sq base, patterned insert	45.00	45.00	—	—	—
Ivy bowl, 6-1/2" d, sq foot, crimp top	35.00	45.00	—	—	—
Juice tumbler, 7 oz, round foot	27.50	27.50	—	—	—
Juice tumbler, 7 oz, sq foot	6.50	6.50	—	—	—
Lamp shade, 17" d	175.00	165.00	—	—	—
Lamp, 6-1/2" h, electric	45.00	45.00	50.00	—	50.00
Lamp, 9-1/2" d, electric	45.00	45.00	115.00	—	115.00
Lamp, candlestick	32.00	32.00	—	—	—
Loving cup, two handles, ftd, 8" d, 6" h	—	—	—	95.00	—
Marmalade, cov	40.00	40.00	45.00	—	70.00
Mayonnaise, 6"	12.00	12.00	22.00	—	22.00
Mustard, cov, sq, foot	18.00	18.00	—	—	—
Nappy, 4-1/2" d, round	8.00	8.00	15.00	30.00	15.00
Nappy, 4-1/2" w, sq	8.50	8.50	—	—	—
Nappy, 5" d, round	10.00	10.00	15.00	35.00	15.00
Nappy, 5-1/2" d, bell	12.00	12.00	—	—	—
Nappy, 6" d, round	10.00	10.00	17.50	—	17.50
Nappy, 6" d, sq	10.00	10.00	17.50	—	17.50
Nappy, 6-1/2" d, round	12.50	12.50	20.00	—	20.00
Nappy, 6-1/2" d, sq	14.00	14.00	—	—	—
Nappy, 7" d, round	14.00	14.00	24.00	—	24.00
Nappy, 7-1/2" d, bell	15.00	15.00	—	—	—
Nappy, 8" d, cupped	22.00	22.00	30.00	—	30.00
Nappy, 8" d, round	22.00	22.00	35.00	—	35.00
Nappy, 9" d, bell	25.00	25.00	—	—	—
Nut, individual, ftd †	6.00	8.00	14.50	—	20.00
Oil bottle, 2 oz, handle	25.00	25.00	—	—	—
Oil bottle, 6 oz, handle	27.50	27.50	—	—	—
Old fashioned tumbler, 5 oz	15.00	15.00	—	—	—
Oyster cocktail, 5 oz, sq foot	12.00	12.00	17.50	—	17.50
Parfait, round foot	17.50	17.50	—	—	—
Pickle, 8" d †	15.00	15.00	—	—	—
Pitcher, 23 oz, rounded	48.00	48.00	150.00	—	165.00
Pitcher, 32 oz, straight side	50.00	50.00	175.00	—	175.00
Pitcher, 38 oz, rounded	65.00	65.00	215.00	—	215.00
Pitcher, 60 oz, rounded	70.00	70.00	295.00	—	295.00
Pitcher, 64 oz, straight side	75.00	75.00	310.00	—	310.00
Plate, 5-1/2" d, round	7.00	7.00	10.00	—	10.00
Plate, 6" w, sq	5.00	5.00	—	—	—

Item	Amber	Crystal	Green	Ice Blue	Pink
Plate, 6-1/2" d, round	6.25	6.25	10.00	—	10.00
Plate, 6-1/2" d, round, depressed center	6.00	6.00	—	—	—
Plate, 8" d, round	9.00	9.00	14.00	—	14.00
Plate, 8" d, round, ftd	13.00	13.00	—	—	—
Plate, 8-1/2" d, plain edge	9.00	9.00	—	—	—
Plate, 8-1/2" d, round	7.00	9.00	17.50	—	28.00
Plate, 8-3/4" w, sq	9.25	9.25	—	—	—
Plate, 10" d, round	15.00	15.00	45.00	—	65.00
Plate, 10" w, sq	15.00	15.00	—	—	—
Plate, 10-1/2" d, round, grill	18.00	18.00	—	—	—
Plate, 12" w, sq	20.00	20.00	—	—	—
Plate, 15" w, sq	28.00	28.00	—	—	—
Preserve, 8" d	15.00	15.00	—	—	—
Puff box, cov, 6" d, round	20.00	20.00	47.50	—	80.00
Punch bowl and stand	215.00	215.00	—	—	—
Punch cup	7.00	7.00	—	—	—
Relish, 8" d, three parts	18.00	18.00	—	—	—
Rose bowl, 4" d	17.50	17.50	48.00	—	50.00
Rose bowl, 6" d	20.00	20.00	—	—	—
Salt and pepper shakers, pr, round foot	27.50	27.50	150.00	—	165.00
Salt and pepper shakers, pr, sq, foot	20.00	20.00	—	—	—
Saucer, demitasse, round	10.00	10.00	15.00	—	17.50
Saucer, demitasse, sq	10.00	10.00	—	—	—
Saucer, round	2.00	3.00	6.00	—	6.00
Saucer, sq	2.00	2.00	—	—	—
Sherbet, high, round foot	7.00	10.00	18.00	—	37.50
Sherbet, high, sq foot	8.00	9.50	18.00	—	—
Sherbet, high, two ball, round foot	10.00	10.00	—	—	—
Sherbet, low, one ball, round foot	12.00	10.00	—	—	15.00
Sherbet, low, round foot	12.50	7.00	—	—	—
Sherbet, low, sq foot	6.50	6.00	15.00	—	17.50
Straw jar, 10" h	65.00	60.00	—	—	—
Sundae	9.00	9.00	—	—	—
Sugar, hexagonal, ftd †	9.00	9.00	40.00	—	48.00
Sugar, low, flat	8.00	8.00	45.00	—	—
Sugar, sq foot	9.00	9.00	48.00	—	55.00
Sweetmeat, 5-1/2" d, ball stem	30.00	30.00	—	—	—
Sweetmeat, 8" d, ball stem	40.00	40.00	60.00	—	65.00
Tidbit, two tiers	27.50	24.50	65.00	85.00	80.00
Toilet bottle, 5 oz	25.00	25.00	40.00	65.00	40.00
Torte plate, 14" d, round	35.00	30.00	48.00	—	48.00

Item	Amber	Crystal	Green	Ice Blue	Pink
Torte plate, 20-1/2" round	55.00	50.00	—	—	—
Tumbler, 8 oz, water	10.00	10.00	24.00	—	24.00
Tumbler, 9 oz, round, ball, water	10.00	10.00	—	—	—
Tumbler, 9 oz, round, ftd water	10.00	10.00	—	—	—
Tumbler, 9 oz, sq foot, water	10.00	10.00	—	—	—
Urn, cov, 11" h	35.00	35.00	350.00	—	350.00
Vase, 6-1/2" h, sq foot	24.00	24.00	—	—	—
Vase, 7-1/2" h, flip	27.50	27.50	70.00	—	70.00
Vase, 7-1/2" h, flip jar with cov	55.00	55.00	85.00	—	85.00
Vase, 8" h, sq foot	35.00	35.00	—	—	—
Vase, 8-1/2" h, flared top	40.00	40.00	120.00	—	235.00
Whiskey, 1-1/2 oz	10.00	10.00	—	—	—
Whiskey, 3 oz	12.00	15.00	—	—	—
Wine, 2 oz, round foot	15.00	12.50	—	—	—
Wine, 2 oz, sq ft	24.00	24.00	35.00	—	65.00
Wine, 2-1/2 oz, ball, foot	20.00	20.00	—	—	—

English Hobnail, crystal nappy with handle, **$22.**

English Hobnail, crystal tumbler, **$10.**

Forest Green

Manufactured by Anchor Hocking Glass Company, Lancaster, Ohio, and Long Island City, N.Y., from 1950 to 1957.

Pieces are made only in forest green.

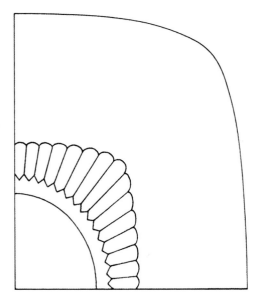

Item	Forest Green	Item	Forest Green
Ashtray, 3-1/4" round	12.00	Plate, 6-3/4" d, salad	7.50
Ashtray, 3-1/2" sq	5.00	Plate, 7" w, sq	6.75
Ashtray, 4-5/8" sq	6.00	Plate, 8-3/8" d, luncheon	9.00
Ashtray, 5-3/4" hexagon	8.00	Plate, 9-1/4" d, dinner	33.50
Ashtray, 5-3/4" sq	7.50	Platter, 11" l, rect	22.00
Batter bowl, spout	25.00	Popcorn bowl, 5-1/4" d	10.00
Berry bowl, large	15.00	Punch bowl	25.00
Berry bowl, small	7.50	Punch bowl and stand	60.00
Bonbon, 6-1/4" w, tricorn	12.00	Punch cup	3.00
Bowl, 4-1/2" w, sq	7.00	Relish tray, 4-3/4" x 6-3/4" l, two	25.00
Bowl, 5-1/4" deep	10.00	handles	
Bowl, 6" w, sq	18.00	Roly Poly tumbler, 5 1/8" h	7.50
Bowl, 6-1/2" d, scalloped	10.00	Salad bowl, 7-3/8" d	15.00
Bowl, 6-3/8" d, three toes	15.00	Sandwich plate, 13-3/4" d	45.00
Bowl, 7-3/8" w, sq	30.00	Saucer, 5-3/8" w	3.00
Bowl, 7-1/2" d, crimped	10.00	Sherbet, 6 oz	9.00
Cocktail, 3-1/2 oz	12.00	Sherbet, 6 oz, Boopie	7.00
Cocktail, 4-1/2 oz	14.00	Sherbet, flat	7.50
Creamer, flat	7.50	Soup bowl, 6" d	17.00
Cup, sq	7.00	Sugar, flat	7.00
Dessert bowl, 4-3/4" d	7.00	Tray, 6" x 10", two handles	30.00
Goblet, 9 oz	10.00	Tumbler, 5 oz, 3-1/2" h	4.00
Goblet, 9-1/2 oz	14.00	Tumbler, 7 oz	4.50
Iced tea tumbler, 13 oz	8.00	Tumbler, 5-1/4" h	7.00
Iced tea tumbler, 14 oz, Boopie	8.00	Tumbler, 9-1/2 oz, tall	8.00
Iced tea tumbler, 15 oz, tall	10.00	Tumbler, 9 oz, fancy	7.00
Iced tea tumbler, 32 oz, giant	18.00	Tumbler, 9 oz, table	5.00
Ivy ball, 4" h	5.00	Tumbler, 10 oz, 4-1/2" h, ftd	8.50
Juice tumbler, 4 oz	10.00	Tumbler, 11 oz	7.00
Juice tumbler, 5-1/2 oz	12.50	Tumbler, 14 oz, 5" h	8.00
Juice Roly Poly tumbler, 3-3/8" h	6.00	Tumbler, 15 oz, long boy	10.00
Ladle, all green glass	80.00	Tumbler, 20 oz, 6-1/4" h	22.00
Mixing bowl, 4-3/4" d, ribbed,	22.00	Vase, 3-1/2" h, ruffled	6.00
crystal lid		Vase, 6-3/8" h, Harding	7.50
Mixing bowl, 6" d	12.00	Vase, 7" h, crimped	15.00
Pitcher, 22 oz	22.50	Vase, 9" h	22.00
Pitcher, 36 oz	25.00	Vegetable bowl, 8-1/2" l, oval	30.00
Pitcher, 86 oz, round	45.00		

Forest Green, cup, **$7**; saucer, **$3.**

Forest Green, deep bowl, 5" d, 4-1/4" deep, **$10.**

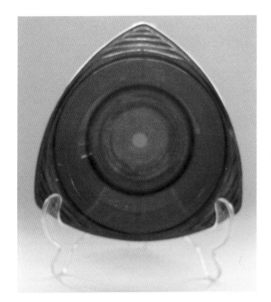

Forest Green, tricorn bon-bon, **$12.**

Forest Green, vase with original foil label, **$22.**

Forest Green, sherbet, Boopie, **$7.**

Fortune

Manufactured by Hocking Glass Company, Lancaster, Ohio, from 1937 to 1938.

Pieces are made in crystal and pink.

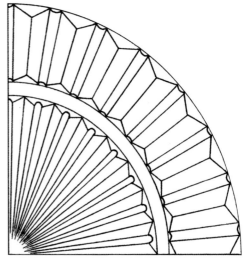

Item	Crystal	Pink
Berry bowl, 4" d	10.00	12.00
Berry bowl, 7-3/4" d	25.00	28.00
Bowl, 4-1/2" d, handle	12.00	15.00
Bowl, 5-1/4" d, rolled edge	20.00	22.00
Candy dish, cov, flat	28.00	30.00
Cup	12.00	15.00
Dessert bowl, 4-1/2" d	12.00	12.00
Juice tumbler, 5 oz, 3-1/2" h	12.00	13.50
Plate, 6" d, sherbet	8.00	15.00
Plate, 8" d, luncheon	25.00	25.00
Salad bowl, 7-3/4" d	25.00	25.00
Saucer	5.00	8.50
Tumbler, 9 oz, 4" h	15.00	16.50

Fortune, pink berry bowl, 7-3/4", **$28.**

Fruits

Manufactured by Hazel Atlas Company, and several other small glass companies, from 1931 to 1935.

Pieces are made in crystal, green, iridized, and pink. Iridized production includes only a 4-inch tumbler, valued at $10.

Item	Crystal	Green	Pink
Berry bowl, 5" d	17.50	32.00	28.00
Berry bowl, 8" d	40.00	85.00	45.00
Console bowl, 7-1/4" d	—	325.00	—
Cup	5.00	12.00	7.00
Juice tumbler, 5 oz, 3-1/2" h	20.00	60.00	22.00
Pitcher, 7" h	50.00	95.00	—
Plate, 8" d, luncheon	12.00	15.00	12.00
Saucer	2.50	6.00	4.50
Sherbet	10.00	15.00	12.00
Tumbler, 4" h, multiple fruits	15.00	24.00	22.00
Tumbler, 4" h, single fruit	20.00	30.00	25.00
Tumbler, 12 oz, 5" h	70.00	200.00	95.00

Fruits, green cup, **$12**; saucer, **$6.**

Fruits, green luncheon plate, **$15.**

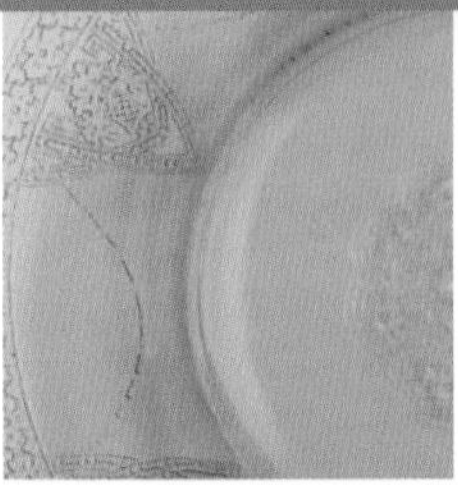

Georgian

Lovebirds

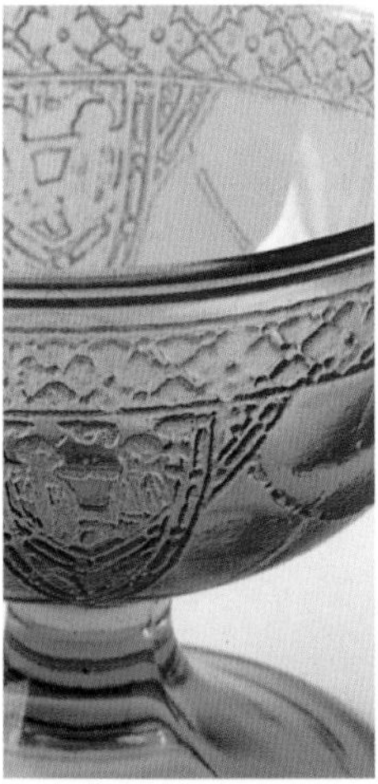

Manufactured by Federal Glass Company, Columbus, Ohio, from 1931 to 1936.

Pieces are made in green. A crystal hot plate is valued at $25.

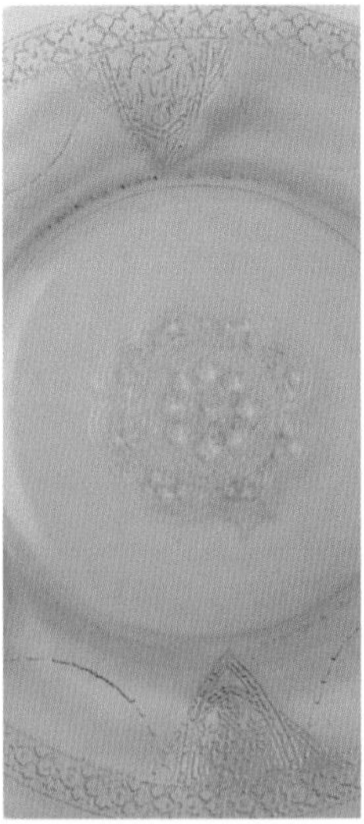

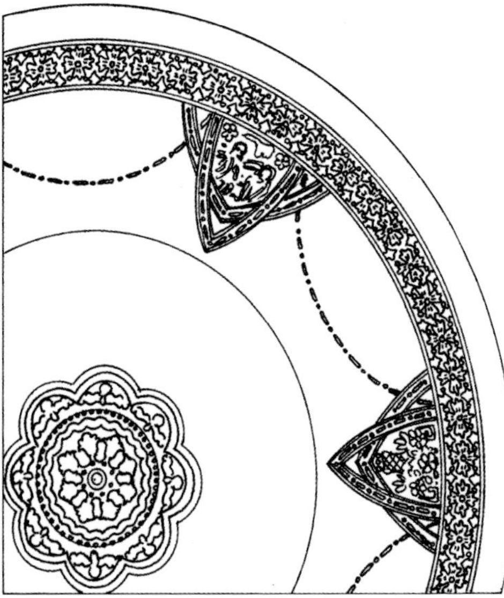

Item	Green
Berry bowl, 4-1/2" d	15.00
Berry bowl, 7-1/2" d, large	65.00
Bowl, 6-1/2" d, deep	65.00
Butter dish, cov	85.00
Cereal bowl, 5-3/4" d	28.50
Cold cuts server, 18-1/2" d, wood, seven openings for 5" d coasters	875.00
Creamer, 3" d, ftd	40.00
Creamer, 4" d, ftd	20.00
Cup	10.00
Hot plate, 5" d, center design	48.00
Plate, 6" d, sherbet	7.50
Plate, 8" d, luncheon	12.00

Item	Green
Plate, 9-1/4" d, center design only	25.00
Plate, 9-1/4" d, dinner	36.00
Platter, 11-1/2" l, closed handle	70.00
Saucer	4.00
Sherbet, ftd	12.00
Sugar cover, 3" d	15.00
Sugar cover, 4" d	15.00
Sugar, 3" d, ftd	35.00
Sugar, 4" d, ftd	35.00
Tumbler, 9 oz, 4" h, flat	65.00
Tumbler 12 oz, 5-1/4" h, flat	125.00
Vegetable bowl, 9" l, oval	65.00

Georgian, green sherbet, **$12.**

Georgian, green luncheon plate, **$12.**

Heritage

Manufactured by Federal Glass Company, Columbus, Ohio, from 1940 to 1955.

Pieces are made in blue, crystal, green, and pink.

Reproductions: † Bowls have been reproduced in amber, crystal, and green. Some are marked with an N or MC.

Item	Blue	Crystal	Green	Pink
Berry bowl, 5" d †	80.00	8.00	75.00	75.00
Berry bowl, 8-1/2" d †	250.00	40.00	200.00	195.00
Creamer, ftd	—	25.00	—	—
Cup	—	7.50	—	—
Fruit bowl, 10-1/2" d	—	15.00	—	—
Plate, 8" d, luncheon	—	9.00	—	—
Plate, 9-1/4" d, dinner	—	12.00	—	—
Sandwich plate, 12" d	—	18.00	—	—
Saucer	—	4.00	—	—
Sugar, open, ftd	—	25.00	—	—

Heritage, crystal dinner plate, **$12.**

Heritage, crystal cup, **$7.50**; saucer, **$4.**

Hex Optic
Honeycomb

Manufactured by Jeannette Glass Company, Jeannette, Pa., from 1928 to 1932.

Pieces are made in green and pink. Ultramarine tumblers have been found. Iridescent tumblers and pitchers were made about 1960 and it is assumed they were made by Jeannette.

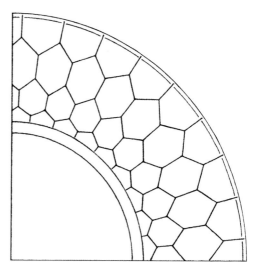

Item	Green	Pink
Berry bowl, 4-1/4" d, ruffled	9.50	8.50
Berry bowl, 7-1/2" d	15.00	12.00
Bucket reamer	65.00	60.00
Butter dish, cov, rect, 1-lb size	90.00	90.00
Creamer, two style handles	8.00	7.00
Cup, two style handles	5.00	5.00
Ice bucket, metal handle	30.00	35.00
Mixing bowl, 7-1/4" d	15.00	15.00
Mixing bowl, 8-1/4" d	18.00	18.00
Mixing bowl, 9" d	20.00	20.00
Mixing bowl, 10" d	20.00	20.00
Pitcher, 32 oz, 5" h	25.00	25.00
Pitcher, 48 oz, 9" h, ftd	48.00	50.00
Pitcher, 96 oz, 8" h	225.00	235.00
Plate, 6" d, sherbet	3.00	3.00
Plate, 8" d, luncheon	6.00	6.00
Platter, 11" d, round	14.00	16.00
Refrigerator dish, 4" x 4"	20.00	18.00
Refrigerator stack set, four pcs	75.00	75.00
Salt and pepper shakers, pr	30.00	50.00
Saucer	4.00	4.00
Sherbet, 5 oz, ftd	5.00	5.00
Sugar, two styles of handles	6.00	6.00
Sugar shaker	225.00	225.00
Tumbler, 12 oz, 5" h	8.00	8.00
Tumbler, 5-3/4" h, ftd	10.00	10.00
Tumbler, 7" h, ftd	15.00	12.00
Tumbler, 7 oz, 4-3/4" h, ftd	8.00	8.00
Tumbler, 9 oz, 3-3/4" h	5.00	5.00
Whiskey, 1 oz, 2" h	8.50	8.50

Hex Optic, green luncheon plate, **$6**; bucket reamer, **$65**.

Hobnail

Manufactured by Hocking Glass Company, Lancaster, Ohio, from 1934 to 1936.

Pieces are made in crystal, crystal with red trim, and pink.

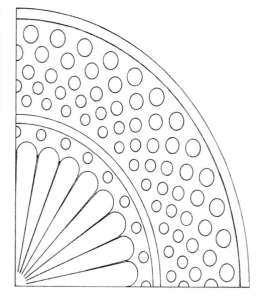

Item	Crystal	Crystal, red trim	Pink
Cereal bowl, 5-1/2" d	4.25	4.25	—
Cordial, 5 oz, ftd	6.00	6.00	—
Creamer, ftd	10.00	4.00	—
Cup	5.00	5.00	10.00
Decanter and stopper, 32 oz	27.50	60.00	—
Goblet, 10 oz	7.50	7.50	—
Iced tea goblet, 13 oz	8.50	8.50	—
Iced tea tumbler, 15 oz	8.50	8.50	—
Juice tumbler, 5 oz	4.00	4.00	—
Milk pitcher, 18 oz	32.50	30.00	—
Pitcher, 67 oz	25.00	25.00	—
Plate, 6" d, sherbet	2.50	2.50	7.50
Plate, 8-1/2" d, luncheon	5.00	5.00	7.50
Salad bowl, 7" d	5.00	5.00	—
Saucer	4.00	4.00	6.00
Sherbet	4.00	4.00	10.00
Sugar, ftd	10.00	8.00	—
Tumbler, 9 oz, 4-3/4" h, flat	5.00	5.00	—
Whiskey, 1-1/2 oz	5.00	5.00	—
Wine, 3 oz, ftd	6.50	6.50	—

Hobnail, pink sherbet, **$10.**

Homespun
Fine Rib

Manufactured by Jeannette Glass Company, Jeannette, Pa., from 1939 to 1949.

Pieces are made in crystal and pink.

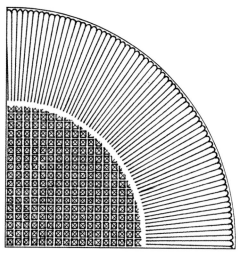

Item	Crystal	Pink
Ashtray	6.00	6.00
Berry bowl, 4-1/2" d, closed handles	15.00	20.00
Berry bowl, 8-1/4" d	20.00	20.00
Butter dish, cov	55.00	90.00
Cereal bowl, 5" d, closed handles	30.00	30.00
Coaster	6.00	6.00
Creamer, ftd	12.50	12.50
Cup	12.00	15.00
Iced tea tumbler, 13 oz, 5-1/4" h	32.00	32.00
Plate, 6" d, sherbet	7.50	12.50
Plate, 9-1/4" d, dinner	18.00	18.00
Platter, 13" d, closed handles	20.00	20.00
Saucer	5.50	10.00
Sherbet, low, flat	17.50	19.00
Sugar, ftd	12.50	12.50
Tumbler, 5 oz, 4" h, ftd	8.00	10.00
Tumbler, 6 oz, 3-7/8" h, straight	7.00	7.50
Tumbler, 9 oz, 4" h, flared top	17.50	17.50
Tumbler, 9 oz, 4-1/4" h, top band	17.50	17.50
Tumbler, 15 oz, 6-1/4" h, ftd	38.00	38.00
Tumbler, 15 oz, 6-3/8" h, ftd	36.00	36.00

Children's

Item	Crystal	Pink
Cup	25.00	35.00
Plate	10.00	185.00
Saucer	9.00	12.00
Teapot	—	125.00

Homespun, pink sugar, **$12.50**; look-alike tumbler.

Horseshoe
No. 612

Manufactured by the Indiana Glass Company, Dunkirk, Ind., from 1930 to 1933.

Pieces are made in crystal, green, pink, and yellow. There is limited collector interest in crystal and pink at the current time.

Item	Green	Yellow
Berry bowl, 4-1/2" d	30.00	25.00
Berry bowl, 9-1/2" d	40.00	35.00
Butter dish, cov	995.00	—
Candy dish, metal holder	175.00	—
Cereal bowl, 6-1/2" d	50.0	35.00
Creamer, ftd	30.00	30.00
Cup and saucer	20.00	28.00
Pitcher, 64 oz, 8-1/2" h	295.00	350.00
Plate, 6" d, sherbet	9.00	10.00
Plate, 8-3/8" d, salad	10.00	18.00
Plate, 9-3/8" d, luncheon	15.00	20.00
Plate, 10-3/8" d, grill	175.00	165.00
Platter, 10-3/4" l, oval	25.00	25.00
Relish, three parts, ftd	40.00	42.50
Salad bowl, 7-1/2" d	24.00	24.00
Sandwich plate, 11-1/2" d	24.00	27.50
Saucer	10.00	10.00
Sherbet	16.00	18.50
Sugar, open	25.00	27.50
Tumbler, 9 oz, ftd	25.00	30.00
Tumbler, 9 oz, 4-1/4" h	150.00	—
Tumbler, 12 oz, ftd	140.00	150.00
Tumbler, 12 oz, 4-3/4" h	150.00	—
Vegetable bowl, 8-1/2" d	30.00	30.00
Vegetable bowl, 10-1/2" d, oval	25.00	50.00

Horseshoe, yellow cup, **$17.50.**

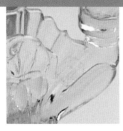

Iris

Iris and Herringbone

Manufactured by Jeannette Glass Company, Jeannette, Pa., from 1928 to 1932 and in the 1950s and 1970s.

Pieces are made in crystal, iridescent, some green, and pink. Recent color combinations of yellow and red and blue and green and white have been made. A record price of $495 is noted for a rare amethyst demitasse cup and saucer.

Reproductions: † Some collectors and dealers feel strongly that the newer re-issues of this pattern are actually reproductions. Forms that have the potential to fool buyers are the 4-1/2-inch berry bowl, covered candy jar, 10-inch diameter dinner plate, 6-1/2-inch high footed tumbler, and vase. Careful examination of the object, plus careful consideration of the color, should help determine age.

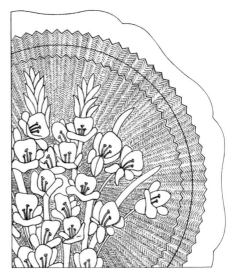

Item	Crystal	Green	Iridescent	Pink
Berry bowl, 4-1/2" d, beaded edge †	60.00	—	32.00	—
Berry bowl, 8" d, beaded edge	125.00	—	30.00	—
Bowl, 5-1/2" d, scalloped	12.00	—	25.00	—
Bowl, 9-1/2" d, scalloped	20.00	—	15.00	—
Bread plate, 11-3/4" d	20.00	—	38.00	—
Butter dish, cov	60.00	—	65.00	—
Candlesticks, pr	45.00	—	50.00	—
Candy jar, cov †	235.00	—	—	—
Cereal bowl, 5" d	140.00	—	—	—
Coaster †	115.00	—	—	—
Cocktail, 4 oz, 4-1/4" h	25.00	—	—	—
Creamer, ftd	12.00	135.00	15.00	150.00
Cup	20.00	—	18.00	—
Demitasse cup and saucer	225.00	—	350.00	—
Fruit bowl, 11" d, straight edge	70.00	—	—	—
Fruit bowl, 11-1/2" d, ruffled	20.00	—	25.00	—
Fruit set	75.00	—	—	—
Goblet, 4 oz, 5-3/4" h	30.00	—	135.00	—
Goblet, 8 oz, 5-3/4" h	30.00	—	175.00	—
Iced tea tumbler, 6-1/2" h, ftd	35.00	—	—	—
Lamp shade, 11-1/2"	100.00	—	—	—
Nut set	115.00	—	—	—
Pitcher, 9-1/2" h, ftd	40.00	—	60.00	—
Plate, 5-1/2" d, sherbet	20.00	—	17.50	—
Plate, 7" d	95.00	—	—	—
Plate, 8" d, luncheon	160.00	—	115.00	—
Plate, 9" d, dinner †	70.00	—	50.00	—
Salad bowl, 9-1/2" d, ruffled	25.00	150.00	20.00	135.00
Sandwich plate, 11-3/4" d	48.00	—	35.00	—
Sauce, 5" d, ruffled	12.50	—	30.00	—
Saucer	18.00	—	12.00	—
Sherbet, 2-1/2" h, ftd	30.00	—	20.00	—
Sherbet, 4" h, ftd	32.00	—	15.50	—
Soup bowl, 7-1/2" d	195.00	—	90.00	—
Sugar, cov	40.00	150.00	25.00	150.00
Tumbler, 4" h, flat †	150.00	—	18.00	—
Tumbler, 6" h, ftd †	25.00	—	22.00	—
Tumbler, 6-1/2" h, ftd †	30.00	—	—	—
Tumbler, flat, water †	165.00	—	—	—
Vase, 9" h †	32.00	—	30.00	225.00
Wine, 4" h	20.00	—	33.50	—
Wine, 4-1/4" h, 3 oz	25.00	—	28.00	—
Wine, 5-1/2" h	25.00	—	—	—

Iris, crystal candlesticks, **$45**; and iridescent plate, **$50.**

Jubilee

Manufactured by Lancaster Glass Company, Lancaster, Ohio, early 1930s.

Pieces are made in pink and yellow.

Item	Pink	Yellow
Bowl, 8" d, 5-1/8" h, three legs	275.00	225.00
Bowl, 11-1/2" d, three legs	265.00	250.00
Bowl, 11-1/2" d, three legs, curved in	—	250.00
Bowl, 13" d, three legs	250.00	245.00
Cake tray, 11" d, two handles	75.00	85.00
Candlesticks, pr	190.00	195.00
Candy jar, cov, three legs	325.00	325.00
Cheese and cracker set	265.00	255.00
Cordial, 1 oz, 4" h	—	245.00
Creamer	45.00	30.00
Cup	40.00	17.50
Fruit bowl, 9" d, handle	—	125.00
Fruit bowl, 11-1/2" h, flat	200.00	165.00
Goblet, 3 oz, 4-7/8" h	—	150.00
Goblet, 11 oz, 7-1/2" h	—	75.00
Iced tea tumbler, 12-1/2 oz, 6-1/8" h	—	135.00
Juice tumbler, 6 oz, 5" h, ftd	—	100.00
Mayonnaise, plate, orig ladle	315.00	285.00
Mayonnaise underplate	125.00	110.00
Plate, 7" d, salad	25.00	16.50
Plate, 8-3/4" d, luncheon	30.00	16.50
Plate, 14" d, three legs	—	210.00
Sandwich plate, 13-1/2" d	95.00	85.00
Sandwich tray, 11" d, center handle	215.00	250.00
Saucer	15.00	6.00
Sherbet, 8 oz, 3" h	—	75.00
Sherbet/champagne, 7 oz, 5-1/2" h	—	75.00
Sugar	40.00	24.00
Tumbler, 10 oz, 6" h, ftd	75.00	40.00
Vase, 12" h	—	385.00

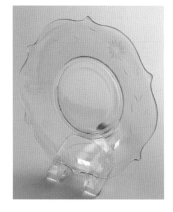

Jubilee, yellow luncheon plate, **$16.50.**

Jubilee, yellow goblet, **$75.**

Jubilee, yellow saucer, **$6**; cup, **$17.50.**

Laced Edge
Katy Blue

Manufactured by Imperial Glass Company, Bellaire, Ohio, early 1930s.

Pieces are made in blue and green and have opalescent edges.

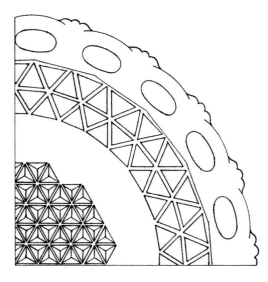

Item	Blue	Green
Basket, 9" d	265.00	—
Bowl, 5" d	40.00	40.00
Bowl, 5-1/2" d	42.00	42.00
Bowl, 5-7/8" d	42.00	42.00
Bowl, 10-1/2" d	60.00	60.00
Bowl, 11" l, oval	295.00	285.00
Bowl, 11" l, oval, divided	165.00	165.00
Candlesticks, pr, double lite	175.00	180.00
Creamer	45.00	40.00
Cup	35.00	35.00
Fruit bowl, 4-1/2" d	32.00	30.00
Mayonnaise, three pieces	100.00	125.00
Plate, 6-1/2" d, bread and butter	24.00	24.00
Plate, 8" d, salad	35.00	35.00
Plate, 10" d, dinner	95.00	95.00
Plate, 12" d, luncheon	90.00	90.00
Platter, 13" l	185.00	165.00
Saucer	18.00	15.00
Soup bowl, 7" d	85.00	80.00
Sugar	45.00	40.00
Tidbit, two tiers, 8" and 10" plates	110.00	100.00
Tumbler, 9 oz	60.00	60.00
Tumbler, 10 oz	62.50	—
Vase, 4-1/2" h	45.00	—
Vase, 5-1/2" h	45.00	—
Vegetable bowl, 9" d	110.00	95.00

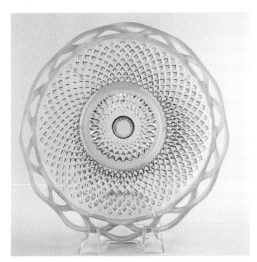

Laced Edge, blue bowl, 5-1/2" d, **$42.**

Lorain

Basket, No. 615

Manufactured by Indiana Glass Company, Dunkirk, Ind., from 1929 to 1939.

Pieces are made in crystal, green, and yellow.

Reproductions: † A fantasy sherbet has been reported in both milk white and avocado green.

Item	Crystal	Green	Yellow
Berry bowl, 8" d	125.00	190.00	250.00
Cereal bowl, 6" d	55.00	65.00	135.00
Creamer, ftd	20.00	20.00	30.00
Cup and saucer	32.00	32.00	25.00
Plate, 5-1/2" d, sherbet	10.00	12.00	15.00
Plate, 7-3/4" d, salad	15.00	18.00	20.00
Plate, 8-3/4" d, luncheon	20.00	24.00	32.50
Plate, 10-1/4" d, dinner	30.00	40.00	90.00
Platter, 11-1/2" l	32.50	32.50	48.00
Relish, 8" d, four parts	20.00	32.00	40.00
Salad bowl, 7-3/4" d	40.00	40.00	75.00
Saucer	6.00	6.00	8.00
Sherbet, ftd †	32.00	20.00	40.00
Snack tray, crystal trim	32.00	37.50	—
Sugar, ftd	20.00	24.00	30.00
Tumbler, 9 oz, 4-3/4" h, ftd	32.00	35.00	35.00
Vegetable bowl, 9-3/4" l, oval	50.00	60.00	65.00

Lorain, yellow luncheon plate, **$32.50**; tumbler, **$35.**

Madrid

Manufactured by Federal Glass Company, Lancaster, Ohio, from 1932 to 1939.

Pieces are made in amber, blue, crystal, green, iridescent, and pink. Iridized pieces are limited to a console set, consisting of a low bowl and pair of candlesticks, valued at $40.

Reproductions: † Reproductions include candlesticks, cups, saucers and a vegetable bowl. Reproductions are found in amber, blue, crystal, and pink. Federal Glass Company reissued this pattern under the name "Recollection." Some of these pieces were dated 1976. When Federal went bankrupt, the molds were sold to Indiana Glass, which removed the date and began production of crystal, then pink. Several pieces were made recently that were not part of the original production and include a footed cake stand, goblet, two-section grill plate, preserves stand, squatty salt and pepper shakers, and 11-ounce tumbler and vase.

Item	Amber	Blue	Crystal	Green	Pink
Ashtray, 6" sq	300.00	—	—	295.00	—
Berry bowl, small	10.00	—	6.50	—	—
Berry bowl, 9-3/8" d	25.00	—	25.00	—	25.00
Bowl, 7" d	17.50	—	12.00	17.50	—
Butter dish, cov	85.00	—	65.00	90.00	—
Cake plate, 11-1/4" d	24.00	—	20.00	—	20.00
Candlesticks, 2-1/4" h, pr †	18.50	—	14.50	—	28.00
Coaster, 5" d	40.00	—	40.00	35.00	—
Console bowl, 11" d	15.00	—	18.00	—	36.00
Cookie jar	50.00	—	45.00	—	40.00
Creamer	30.00	18.00	7.00	20.00	—
Cream soup, 4 3/4" d	25.00	—	15.50	—	—
Cup †	10.00	20.00	6.50	12.00	8.50
Gelatin mold, 2-1/2" h	25.00	—	20.00	—	—
Gravy boat	1,950.00	—	900.00	—	—
Gravy boat platter	900.00	—	900.00	—	—
Hot dish coaster, 3-1/2" d	195.00	—	40.00	45.00	—
Iced tea tumbler, round	25.00	—	24.00	22.00	—
Jam dish, 7" d	24.00	35.00	12.00	25.00	—
Jello, 2" h	18.00	—	—	—	—
Juice pitcher	50.00	—	45.00	—	—
Juice tumbler, 5 oz, 3-7/8" h, ftd	18.00	45.00	40.00	35.00	—
Pitcher, jug-type	60.00	—	24.00	190.00	—
Pitcher, 60 oz, 8" h, sq	55.00	225.00	150.00	145.00	50.00
Pitcher, 80 oz, 8-1/2" h, ice lip	75.00	—	30.00	225.00	—
Plate, 6" d, sherbet	5.50	12.00	4.00	4.50	4.00
Plate, 7-1/2" d, salad	15.00	17.00	12.00	9.00	9.00
Plate, 8-7/8" d, luncheon	10.00	20.00	7.50	12.00	10.00
Plate, 10-1/2" d, dinner	48.00	60.00	24.00	45.00	—
Plate, 10-1/2" d, grill	12.00	—	10.00	18.50	—
Platter, 11-1/2" oval	20.00	32.00	20.00	18.00	18.00
Relish dish, 10-1/2" d	14.50	—	7.00	16.00	20.00
Salad bowl, 8" d	17.00	—	9.50	15.50	—
Salad bowl, 9-1/2" d	32.00	—	30.00	—	—
Salt and pepper shakers, 3-1/2" h	135.00	145.00	95.00	110.00	—
Sauce bowl, 5" d	12.00	—	7.50	8.50	11.00
Saucer †	5.00	8.00	4.00	7.00	5.00
Sherbet, cone	5.50	18.00	6.50	14.00	—
Sherbet, ftd	10.00	15.00	6.00	12.00	—
Soup bowl, 7" d †	20.00	20.00	6.00	15.50	—
Sugar, cov †	65.00	175.00	32.50	80.00	—
Sugar, open †	20.00	15.00	8.00	20.00	—
Tumbler, 9 oz, 4-1/2" h	18.00	40.00	17.50	25.00	22.50
Tumbler, 12 oz, 5-1/4" h, ftd or flat	30.00	—	30.00	45.00	—
Vegetable bowl, 10" l, oval †	30.00	35.00	25.00	25.00	30.00

Madrid, amber grill plate, **$12**; berry bowl, **$10**; cup, **$10**.

Madrid, amber sugar, **$20**; creamer, **$30**.

Madrid, amber bowl, **$17.50**.

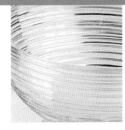

Manhattan
Horizontal Ribbed

Manufactured by Anchor Hocking Glass Company, from 1938 to 1943.

Pieces are made in crystal, green, iridized, pink, and ruby. Ruby pieces are limited to relish tray inserts, currently valued at $8 each. Green and iridized production was limited to footed tumblers, currently valued at $17.50. Anchor Hocking introduced a similar pattern, Park Avenue, in 1987. Anchor Hocking was careful to preserve the Manhattan pattern. Collectors should pay careful attention to measurements if they are uncertain of the pattern.

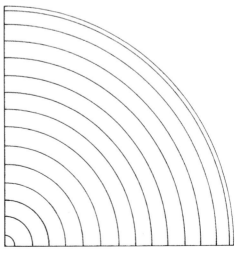

Item	Crystal	Pink
Ashtray, 4" d, round	15.00	10.00
Ashtray, 4-1/2" w, sq	20.00	—
Berry bowl, 5-3/8" d, handles	24.00	25.00
Berry bowl, 7-1/2" d	28.00	—
Bowl, 4-1/2" d	12.50	—
Bowl, 8" d, closed handles	28.00	25.00
Bowl, 8" d, metal handle	35.00	—
Bowl, 9-1/2" d, handle	—	45.00
Candlesticks, pr, 4-1/2" h	20.00	—
Candy dish, three legs	—	18.00
Candy dish, cov	40.00	—
Cereal bowl, 5-1/4" d, no handles	120.00	—
Coaster, 3-1/2"	30.00	—
Cocktail	18.00	—
Comport, 5-3/4" h	35.00	60.00
Creamer, oval	9.00	20.00
Cup	22.00	160.00
Fruit bowl, 9-1/2" d, two open handles	40.00	50.00
Juice pitcher, 24 oz	55.00	—
Pitcher, 80 oz, tilted	55.00	85.00
Plate, 6" d, sherbet	12.00	50.00
Plate, 8-1/2" d, salad	20.00	—
Plate, 10-1/4" d, dinner	25.00	120.00
Relish tray insert	2.50	10.00
Relish tray, 14" d, inserts	110.00	50.00
Relish tray, 14" d, four parts	85.00	—
Salad bowl, 9" d	20.00	—
Salt and pepper shakers, pr, 2" h, sq	30.00	60.00
Sandwich plate, 14" d	22.00	—
Sauce bowl, 4-1/2" d, handles	10.00	—
Saucer	7.00	50.00
Sherbet	12.50	20.00
Sugar, oval	15.00	17.50
Tumbler, 10 oz, 5-1/4" h, ftd	20.00	27.50
Vase, 8" h	25.00	—
Wine, 3-1/2" h	8.00	—

Manhattan, small crystal bowl (on pedestal), **$9**; pink creamer, **$20,** and sugar, **$17.50;** crystal salt and pepper shakers, **$30;** crystal iced tea tumbler, **$20;** crystal pitcher, **$55;** relish with metal stand, **$30;** and pink footed candy dish, **$18.**

Manhattan, relish tray with ruby inserts and crystal base, **$110;** and crystal comport, **$35.**

Manhattan, vase, **$25**; and fruit bowl with open handles, **$40.**

Mayfair
Federal

Manufactured by Federal Glass Company, Columbus, Ohio, 1934.

Pieces are made in amber, crystal, and green.

Item	Amber	Crystal	Green
Cereal bowl, 6" d	18.50	15.00	22.00
Cream soup, 5" d	22.00	12.00	20.00
Creamer, ftd	17.50	14.00	16.00
Cup	8.50	5.00	8.50
Plate, 6-3/4" d, salad	7.00	4.50	8.50
Plate, 9-1/2" d, dinner	16.50	12.00	14.50
Plate, 9-1/2" d, grill	17.50	15.00	17.50
Platter, 12" l, oval	27.50	22.00	30.00
Sauce bowl, 5" d	8.50	7.00	12.00
Saucer	4.50	2.50	4.50
Sugar, ftd	12.00	10.00	12.00
Tumbler, 9 oz, 4-1/2" h	27.50	16.50	32.00
Vegetable, 10" l, oval	32.00	32.00	32.00

Mayfair Federal, amber dinner plate, **$16.50.**

Mayfair
Open Rose

Manufactured by Hocking Glass Company, Lancaster, Ohio, from 1931 to 1937.

Pieces are made in crystal, green, ice blue, pink, and yellow.

Reproductions: † This pattern has been plagued with reproductions since 1977. Items reproduced include cookie jars, salt and pepper shakers, juice pitchers, and whiskey glasses. Reproductions are found in amethyst, blue, cobalt blue, green, pink, and red.

Item	Crystal	Green	Ice Blue	Pink	Pink Satin	Yellow
Bowl, 11-3/4" l, flat	—	35.00	75.00	85.00	70.00	195.00
Butter dish, cov	—	1,295.00	350.00	80.00	95.00	1,295.00
Cake plate, 10" d, ftd	—	115.00	90.00	40.00	45.00	—
Cake plate, 12" d, handles	—	40.00	95.00	50.00	50.00	—
Candy dish, cov	—	575.00	325.00	70.00	85.00	475.00
Celery dish, 9" l, divided	—	155.00	75.00	—	—	150.00
Celery dish, 10" l, divided	—	—	90.00	295.00	—	—
Celery dish, 10" l, not divided	—	115.00	80.00	65.00	50.00	115.00
Cereal bowl, 5-1/2" d	—	24.00	48.00	35.00	35.00	75.00
Claret, 4-1/2 oz, 5-1/4" h	—	950.00	—	1,150.00	—	—
Cocktail, 3 oz, 4" h	—	975.00	—	130.00	—	—
Console bowl, 9" d, 3-1/8" h, three legs	—	5,000.00	—	5,000.00	—	—
Cookie jar, cov †	—	575.00	295.00	75.00	37.00	860.00
Cordial, 1 oz, 3-3/4" h	—	950.00	—	1,100.00	—	—
Cream soup, 5" d	—	—	—	65.00	68.00	—
Creamer, ftd	—	—	—	40.00	30.00	—
Cup	—	150.00	55.00	20.00	27.50	150.00
Decanter, stopper, 32 oz	—	—	—	275.00	—	—
Fruit bowl, 12" d, scalloped	—	50.00	125.00	95.00	75.00	215.00
Goblet, 2-1/2 oz, 4-1/8"	—	950.00	—	950.00	—	—
Goblet, 9 oz, 5-3/4" h	—	465.00	—	80.00	—	—
Goblet, 9 oz, 7-1/4" h, thin	—	—	225.00	475.00	—	—
Iced tea tumbler, 13-1/2 oz, 5-1/4" h	—	—	225.00	80.00	—	—
Iced tea tumbler, 15 oz, 6-1/2" h, ftd	—	250.00	285.00	45.00	65.00	—
Juice pitcher, 37 oz, 6" h †	24.50	525.00	150.00	85.00	65.00	525.00
Juice tumbler, 3 oz, 3-1/4" h, ftd	—	—	—	80.00	—	—
Juice tumbler, 5 oz, 3-1/2"	—	—	225.00	85.00	—	—
Pitcher, 60 oz, 8" h	—	475.00	195.00	85.00	100.00	425.00
Pitcher, 80 oz, 8-1/2" h	—	725.00	225.00	135.00	135.00	725.00
Plate, 5-3/4" d	—	90.00	25.00	20.00	15.00	90.00
Plate, 6-1/2" d, off-center indent	—	115.00	44.00	30.00	35.00	—
Plate, 6-1/2" d, sherbet	—	—	24.00	20.00	—	—
Plate, 8-1/2" d, luncheon	—	85.00	70.00	35.00	35.00	80.00
Plate, 9-1/2" d, dinner	—	150.00	100.00	70.00	65.00	150.00
Plate, 9-1/2" d, grill	—	75.00	70.00	50.00	35.00	80.00
Plate, 11-1/2" d, grill, handles	—	—	—	—	—	100.00

Item	Crystal	Green	Ice Blue	Pink	Pink Satin	Yellow
Platter, 12" l, oval, open handles	17.50	175.00	60.00	35.00	35.00	115.00
Platter, 12-1/2" oval, 8" wide, closed handles	—	245.00	—	—	—	245.00
Relish, 8-3/8" d, four parts	—	160.00	65.00	37.50	37.50	160.00
Relish, 8-3/8" d, non-partitioned	—	275.00	—	200.00	—	275.00
Salt and pepper shakers, pr, flat †	20.00	1,000.00	175.00	65.00	70.00	800.00
Sandwich server, center handle	—	40.00	85.00	50.00	50.00	130.00
Saucer	—	90.00	30.00	45.00	35.00	140.00
Sherbet, 2-1/4" flat	—	—	135.00	185.00	—	—
Sherbet, 3" ftd	—	—	—	20.00	—	—
Sherbet, 4-3/4" ftd	—	150.00	75.00	185.00	75.00	150.00
Sugar, ftd	—	195.00	85.00	38.00	40.00	185.00
Sweet pea vase	—	285.00	150.00	250.00	145.00	—
Tumbler, 9 oz, 4-1/4" h	—	—	100.00	30.00	—	—
Tumbler, 10 oz, 5-1/4" h	—	—	145.00	65.00	—	185.00
Tumbler, 11 oz, 4-3/4" h	—	200.00	250.00	225.00	225.00	215.00
Vase	—	—	175.00	295.00	—	—
Vegetable bowl, 7" d, two handles	—	33.00	75.00	60.00	70.00	195.00
Vegetable bowl, 9-1/2" l, oval	—	110.00	70.00	45.00	30.00	125.00
Vegetable bowl, 10" d cov	—	—	120.00	150.00	120.00	900.00
Vegetable bowl, 10" d open	—	—	85.00	48.50	20.00	200.00
Whiskey, 1-1/2 oz, 2-1/4" h †	—	—	—	58.00	—	—

Mayfair Open Rose, blue handled vegetable bowl, **$60.**

REPRODUCTION! Mayfair Open Rose, green and blue cookie jars.

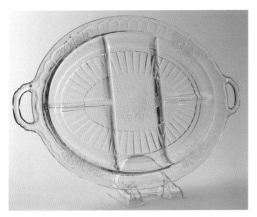

Mayfair Open Rose, crystal platter, open handles, **$17.50.**

Mayfair Open Rose, pink tumbler, 11 oz, **$225**; pink satin-finish covered cookie jar, **$37.**

Miss America
Diamond Pattern

Manufactured by Hocking Glass Company, Lancaster, Ohio, from 1935 to 1938.

Pieces are made in crystal, green, ice blue, jade-ite, pink, and royal ruby.

Reproductions: † Reproductions include the butter dish (including a new importer), creamer, 8-inch pitcher, salt and pepper shakers, sugar, and tumbler. Reproductions are found in amberina, blue, cobalt blue, crystal, green, pink, and red.

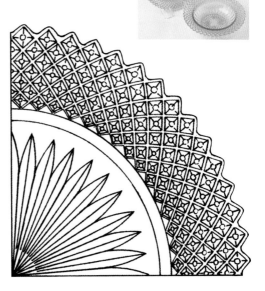

Miss America, green salad plate, **$14**; berry bowl, **$25**.

Item	Crystal	Green	Ice Blue	Pink	Royal Ruby
Berry bowl, 4-1/2" d	—	25.00	—	—	—
Bowl, 8" d, curved at top	48.00	—	—	95.00	—
Bowl, 8" d, straight sides	—	—	—	110.00	—
Bowl, 11" d, shallow	—	—	—	—	850.00
Butter dish, cov †	300.00	—	—	575.00	—
Cake plate, 12" d, ftd	40.00	—	—	45.00	—
Candy jar, cov, 11-1/2"	125.00	—	—	200.00	—
Celery dish, 10-1/2" l, oval	19.50	—	160.00	45.00	—
Cereal bowl, 6-1/4" d	15.00	18.00	—	35.00	—
Coaster, 5-3/4" d	19.50	—	—	45.00	—
Comport, 5" d	18.00	—	—	50.00	—
Creamer, ftd †	12.50	—	—	24.00	215.00
Cup	11.00	20.00	14.00	30.00	235.00
Fruit bowl, 8-3/4" d	40.00	—	—	60.00	450.00
Goblet, 10 oz, 5-1/2" h	30.00	—	—	75.00	250.00
Iced tea tumbler, 14 oz, 5-3/4" h	25.00	—	—	85.00	—
Juice goblet, 5 oz, 4-3/4" h	35.00	—	—	115.00	250.00
Juice tumbler, 5 oz, 4" h	27.50	—	150.00	60.00	200.00
Pitcher, 65 oz, 8" h †	45.00	—	—	175.00	—
Pitcher, 65 oz, 8-1/2" h, ice lip	75.00	—	—	295.00	50.00
Plate, 5-3/4" d, sherbet	10.00	9.00	55.00	16.00	—
Plate, 6-3/4" d	—	12.00	—	—	—
Plate, 8-1/2" d, salad	15.00	14.00	—	60.00	150.00
Plate, 10-1/4" d, dinner	25.00	—	150.00	45.00	—
Plate, 10-1/4" d, grill	12.00	—	—	50.00	—
Platter, 12-1/4" l, oval	18.00	—	—	95.00	—
Relish, 8-3/4" l, 4 part	30.00	—	—	30.00	—
Relish, 11-3/4" d, divided	50.00	—	—	40.00	—
Salt and pepper shakers, pr †	40.00	300.00	—	95.00	—
Saucer	4.00	—	—	10.00	60.00
Sherbet	12.50	—	60.00	35.00	175.00
Sugar †	12.00	—	—	40.00	225.00
Tumbler, 10 oz, 4-1/2" h, flat †	25.00	35.00	—	80.00	—
Tumbler, 14 oz, 5-3/4" h	28.00	—	—	—	—
Vegetable bowl, 10" l, oval	20.00	—	—	70.00	—
Whiskey	24.00	—	—	—	—
Wine, 3 oz, 3-3/4" h	25.00	—	—	85.00	250.00

Miss America, pink goblet, **$75**; comport, **$50**; and 10-oz tumbler with original label, **$80**.

Moderntone

Manufactured by Hazel Atlas Glass Company, Clarksburg, W.V., and Zanesville, Ohio, from 1934 to 1942; also, in the late 1940s to early 1950s.

Pieces are made in amethyst, cobalt blue, crystal, pink, and Platonite fired-on colors. Later period production saw plain white, as well as white with blue or red stripes, a Willow-type design in blue or red on white. Collector interest in crystal is limited and prices remain low, less than 50 percent of Platonite.

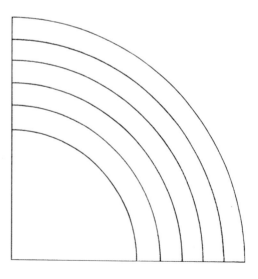

Item	Amethyst	Cobalt Blue	Platonite, Darker Shades	Platonite, Pastel Shades	White or White with Dec	Willow-Type Dec
Ashtray, 7-3/4" d, match holder center	—	185.00	—	—	—	—
Berry bowl, 5" d, rim	25.00	35.00	—	7.00	5.00	15.00
Berry bowl, 5" d, without rim	—	—	12.50	25.00	—	—
Berry bowl, 8-3/4" d	42.00	50.00	—	—	7.50	28.00
Bowl, 8" d, no rim	—	—	40.00	50.00	—	—
Bowl, 8" d, rim	—	—	—	15.00	6.00	28.00
Butter dish, metal cov	—	95.00	—	—	—	—
Cereal bowl, 5" d, deep, no white	—	—	17.50	10.00	—	—
Cereal bowl, 5" deep, with white	—	—	—	9.00	4.50	—
Cereal bowl, 6-1/2" d	70.00	70.00	—	—	—	—
Cheese dish, 7" d, metal cov	—	475.00	—	—	—	—
Cream soup, 4-3/4" d	25.00	25.00	—	12.00	9.00	25.00
Cream soup, 5" d, ruffled	25.00	85.00	—	—	—	—
Creamer	18.00	13.50	12.00	5.50	4.50	20.00
Cup	12.00	18.00	10.00	6.00	2.50	22.00
Custard cup	18.00	20.00	—	—	—	—
Mug, 4" h, 8 oz	—	—	—	—	8.50	—
Mustard, metal lid	—	25.00	—	—	—	—
Plate, 5-7/8" d, sherbet	5.50	10.00	—	—	—	—
Plate, 6-3/4" d, salad	12.50	12.50	12.00	10.00	6.00	10.00
Plate, 7-3/4" d, luncheon	10.00	18.00	—	—	—	—
Plate, 8-7/8" d, dinner	12.00	20.00	20.00	12.00	4.00	20.00
Platter, 11" l, oval	40.00	55.00	—	—	14.00	30.00
Platter, 12" l, oval	48.00	165.00	32.00	15.00	10.00	35.00
Salt and pepper shakers, pr	45.00	50.00	—	10.00	12.00	—
Sandwich plate, 10-1/2" d	35.00	75.00	—	20.00	12.50	—
Saucer	4.50	5.00	7.50	3.50	3.50	4.50
Sherbet	13.00	15.00	12.00	8.00	4.50	14.00
Soup bowl, 7-1/2" d	95.00	195.00	—	—	—	—
Sugar	18.00	15.00	12.00	6.00	4.50	20.00
Tumbler, 5 oz	40.00	55.00	—	—	—	—
Tumbler, 9 oz	30.00	40.00	45.00	12.00	—	—
Tumbler, 12 oz	85.00	95.00	—	—	—	—
Tumbler, cone, ftd	—	—	—	—	4.00	—
Whiskey, 1-1/2 oz	—	45.00	—	18.50	—	—

Children's

Hazel Atlas also manufactured children's sets in the early 1950s, known as Little Hostess Party Dishes. The original box adds to the value. Colorful combinations were found.

Item	Gray/ Rust/ Gold	Green/ Gray/ Chartreuse	Lemon/ Beige/ Pink/Aqua	Pastel Pink/ Green/Blue/ Yellow	Pink/ Black/ White
Creamer, 1-3/4"	12.50	16.00	15.00	15.00	15.00
Cup, 3/4"	15.00	12.00	12.00	13.50	15.00
Plate, 5-1/4" d	15.00	10.00	12.00	10.00	12.00
Saucer, 3-7/8" d	8.00	7.00	12.50	7.00	7.00
Sugar, 1-3/4"	12.00	15.00	20.00	15.00	18.00
Teapot, 3-1/2" d	125.00	115.00	95.00	—	95.00

Moderntone (children's), darker shades of Platonite saucers, **$7.50** each.

Moderntone, cobalt blue dinner plate, **$20**; salad plate, **$12.50**; sherbet (on pedestal), **$15**; cup, **$18**, and saucer, **$5**; cream soup, **$25.**

Moondrops

Manufactured by New Martinsville Glass Company, New Martinsville, W.V., from 1932 to 1940.

Pieces are made in amber, amethyst, black, cobalt blue, crystal, dark green, green, ice blue, Jade-ite, light green, pink, red, and smoke.

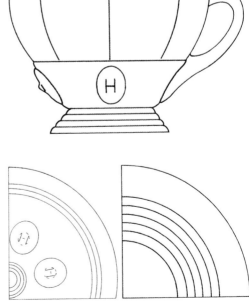

Item	Cobalt Blue	Crystal	Other Colors	Red
Ashtray	30.00	—	18.00	35.00
Berry bowl, 5-1/4" d	20.00	—	12.00	20.00
Bowl, 8-1/2" d, ftd, concave top	40.00	—	25.00	40.00
Bowl, 9-1/2" d, three legs, ruffled	60.00	—	—	60.00
Bowl, 9-3/4" l, oval, handles	50.00	—	30.00	50.00
Butter dish, cov	425.00	—	275.00	295.00
Candlesticks, pr, 2" h, ruffled	40.00	—	25.00	40.00
Candlesticks, pr, 4" h, sherbet style	30.00	—	18.00	30.00
Candlesticks, pr, 5" h, ruffled	32.00	—	22.00	32.00
Candlesticks, pr, 5" h, wings	90.00	—	60.00	90.00
Candlesticks, pr, 5-1/4" h, triple light	100.00	65.00	65.00	100.00
Candlesticks, pr, 8-1/2" h, metal stem	40.00	—	32.00	40.00
Candy dish, 8" d, ruffled	40.00	—	20.00	40.00
Casserole, cov, 9-3/4" d	185.00	—	100.00	185.00
Celery bowl, 11" l, boat-shape	30.00	—	24.00	30.00
Cocktail shaker, metal top	60.00	—	35.00	60.00
Comport, 4" d	25.00	—	15.00	25.00
Comport, 11-1/2" d	60.00	—	30.00	60.00
Console bowl, 12" d, round, three ftd	—	—	40.00	—
Console bowl, 13" d, wings	—	—	80.00	120.00
Cordial, 3/4 oz, 2-7/8" h	55.00	—	25.00	48.00
Cream soup, 4-1/4" d	90.00	—	35.00	90.00
Creamer, 2-3/4" h	15.00	—	10.00	25.00
Creamer, 3-3/4" h	12.00	—	12.00	16.00
Cup	16.00	8.00	10.00	16.00
Decanter, 7-3/4" h	70.00	—	40.00	70.00
Decanter, 8-1/2" h	72.00	—	45.00	72.00
Decanter, 10-1/4" h, rocket-shape	425.00	—	375.00	425.00
Decanter, 11-1/4" h	100.00	—	50.00	110.00
Goblet, 5 oz, 4-3/4" h	25.00	—	15.00	22.00
Goblet, 8 oz, 5-3/4" h	35.00	—	20.00	33.00
Goblet, 9 oz, 6-1/4" h, metal stem	15.00	—	17.50	15.00
Gravy boat	120.00	—	90.00	125.00
Juice tumbler, 3 oz, 3-1/4" h, ftd	15.00	—	10.00	18.00
Mayonnaise, 5-1/4" h	32.50	—	30.00	32.50
Mug, 12 oz, 5-1/8" h	40.00	—	24.00	42.00
Perfume bottle, rocket-shape	200.00	—	150.00	210.00
Pickle, 7-1/2" d	25.00	—	15.00	25.00
Pitcher, 22 oz, 6-7/8" h	175.00	—	90.00	175.00
Pitcher, 32 oz, 8-1/8" h	195.00	—	110.00	195.00
Pitcher, 50 oz, 8" h, lip	200.00	—	115.00	200.00
Pitcher, 53 oz, 8-1/8" h	195.00	—	120.00	195.00
Plate, 5-7/8" d	12.00	—	7.50	12.00
Plate, 6" d, round, off center indent	12.50	—	10.00	12.50
Plate, 6-1/8" d, sherbet	8.00	—	6.00	8.00

Item	Cobalt Blue	Crystal	Other Colors	Red
Plate, 7-1/8" d, salad	12.00	—	10.00	12.00
Plate, 8-1/2" d, luncheon	20.00	—	12.00	15.00
Plate, 9-1/2" d, dinner	25.00	—	15.00	25.00
Platter, 12" l, oval	35.00	—	20.00	35.00
Powder jar, three ftd	175.00	—	100.00	185.00
Relish, 8-1/2" d, 3 ftd, divided	30.00	—	20.00	30.00
Sandwich plate, 14" d	40.00	—	20.00	40.00
Sandwich plate, 14" d, with handles	44.00	—	24.00	45.00
Saucer	6.00	2.00	4.00	8.50
Sherbet, 2-5/8" h	15.00	10.00	11.00	20.00
Sherbet, 3-1/2" h	35.00	—	15.00	25.00
Shot glass, 2 oz, 2-3/4" h	17.50	—	12.00	24.50
Shot glass, 2 oz, 2-3/4" h, handle	17.50	—	12.00	17.50
Soup bowl, 6-3/4" d	80.00	—	—	80.00
Sugar, 2-3/4" h	12.00	—	12.00	20.00
Tray, 7-1/2" l	15.00	—	20.00	16.00
Tumbler, 5 oz, 3-5/8" h	15.00	—	10.00	15.00
Tumbler, 7 oz, 4-3/8" h	17.50	—	10.00	18.00
Tumbler, 8 oz, 4-3/8" h	17.50	—	12.00	22.00
Tumbler, 9 oz, 4-7/8" h, handle	30.00	—	15.00	28.00
Tumbler, 9 oz, 4-7/8" h	20.00	—	15.00	22.00
Tumbler, 12 oz, 5-1/8" h	30.00	—	15.00	35.00
Vase, 7-1/4" h, flat, ruffled	60.00	—	60.00	60.00
Vase, 8-1/2" h, bud, rocket-shape	245.00	—	185.00	245.00
Vase, 9-1/4" h, rocket-shape	240.00	—	125.00	240.00
Vegetable bowl, 9-3/4" l, oval	48.00	—	24.00	48.00
Wine, 3 oz, 5-1/2" h, metal stem	17.50	—	12.00	16.00
Wine, 4-3/4" h, rocket-shape	27.50	—	30.00	85.00
Wine, 4 oz, 4" h	24.00	—	12.00	27.50
Wine, 4 oz, 5-1/2" h, metal stem	20.00	—	12.00	20.00

Above; Moondrops, red sugar, **$20**; creamer, **$16.**
Left: Moondrops, pink saucer, **$4**; cup, **$10.**

Moonstone

Manufactured by Anchor Hocking Glass Company, Lancaster, Ohio, from 1941 to 1946.

Pieces are made in crystal with opalescent hobnails and Ocean Green with opalescent hobnails.

Moonstone, crystal puff box, covered, 4-3/4", **$25**; cigarette box, covered, **$25.**

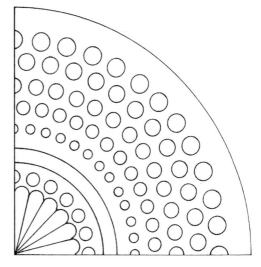

Item	Crystal	Ocean Green
Berry bowl, 5-1/2" d	25.00	—
Bonbon, heart shape, handle	15.00	—
Bowl, 5-1/2" d, ruffled	10.00	—
Bowl, 6-1/2" d, crimped, handle	20.00	—
Bowl, 9-1/2" d, crimped	25.00	—
Bud vase, 5-1/2" h	18.00	—
Candleholder, pr	20.00	—
Candy jar, cov, 6" h	30.00	—
Cigarette box, cov	25.00	—
Creamer	10.00	9.50
Cup	8.00	10.00
Dessert bowl, 5-1/2" d, crimped	12.50	—
Goblet, 10 oz	20.00	24.00
Plate, 6-1/4" d, sherbet	7.00	9.00
Plate, 8-3/8" d, luncheon	17.50	17.50
Puff box, cov, 4-3/4" d, round	25.00	—
Relish, 7-3/4" d, divided	12.00	—
Relish, cloverleaf	14.00	—
Sandwich plate, 10-3/4" d	45.00	—
Saucer	6.00	6.00
Sherbet, ftd	7.50	7.00
Sugar, ftd	10.00	12.50
Vase, 5-1/2" h	24.00	—

Moonstone, crystal candleholders, pair, **$20.**

Moonstone, crystal bud vase, 5-1/2", **$18.**

Moonstone, crystal sandwich plate, 10-3/4", **$45.**

Moonstone, crystal goblet, **$20**; cup and saucer, **$14;** luncheon plate, 8-1/4", **$17.50.**

Moroccan Amethyst

Manufactured by Hazel Ware, division of Continental Can, 1960s.

Pieces are made in amethyst.

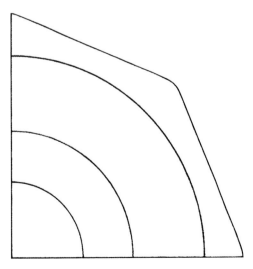

Item	Amethyst	Item	Amethyst
Ashtray, 3-1/4" d, round	5.75	Juice goblet, 5-1/2 oz, 4-3/8" h	12.00
Ashtray, 3-1/4" w, triangular	5.75	Juice tumbler, 4 oz, 2-1/2" h	12.00
Ashtray, 5-3/8" w, triangular	15.00	Old fashioned tumbler, 8 oz, 3-1/4" h	12.50
Ashtray, 6-7/8" w, triangular	12.50		
Ashtray, 8" w, square	14.00	Plate, 5-3/4" d, sherbet	4.50
Bowl, 5-3/4" w, deep, square	12.00	Plate, 7-1/4" d, salad	7.00
Bowl, 6" d, round	12.50	Plate, 9-3/4" d, dinner	9.00
Bowl, 7-3/4" l, oval	168.00	Punch bowl	85.00
Bowl, 7-3/4" l, rectangular	15.00	Punch cup	6.00
Bowl, 7-3/4" l, rectangular, metal handle	17.50	Relish, 7-3/4" l	14.00
		Salad fork and spoon	12.00
Bowl, 9-1/2" x 4-1/4", rectangular	18.00	Sandwich plate, 12" d, metal handle	15.00
Bowl, 10-3/4" d	30.00		
Candy, cov, short	35.00	Saucer	3.00
Candy, cov, tall	32.00	Sherbet, 7-1/2 oz, 4-1/4" h	7.50
Chip and dip, 10-3/4" and 5-3/4" bowls in metal frame	40.00	Snack plate, 10" l, fan shaped, cup rest	8.00
Cocktail shaker, chrome lid	30.00	Snack set, square plate, cup	12.00
Cocktail, stirrer, 16 oz, 6-1/4" h, lip	30.00	Tidbit, three tiers	75.00
		Tumbler, 9 oz	10.00
Cup	7.50	Tumbler, 11 oz, 4-1/4" h, crinkled bottom	12.00
Fruit bowl, 4-3/4" d, octagonal	9.00		
Goblet, 9 oz, 5-1/2" h	12.50	Tumbler, 11 oz, 4-5/8" h	12.00
Ice bucket, 6" h	50.00	Vase, 8-1/2" h, ruffled	40.00
Iced tea tumbler, 16 oz, 6-1/2" h	18.50	Wine, 4-1/2 oz, 4" h	10.00

Moroccan Amethyst, cup, **$7.50**; saucer, **$3.**

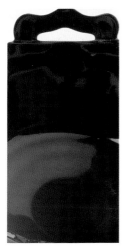

Mt. Pleasant

Manufactured by L.E. Smith, Mt. Pleasant, Pa., from the 1920s to 1934.

Pieces are made in amethyst, black, cobalt blue, crystal, green, pink, and white.

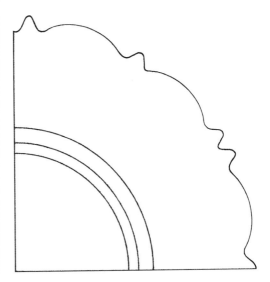

Item	Amethyst	Black	Cobalt Blue	Green	Pink
Bonbon, 7" d, rolled edge	24.00	24.50	24.00	16.00	16.00
Bowl, 6" d, three legs	—	25.00	—	—	—
Bowl, 6" w, sq, two handles	27.50	18.00	24.00	15.00	15.00
Bowl, 7" d, three ftd, rolled out edge	18.50	24.50	18.50	17.50	17.50
Bowl, 8" d, scalloped, two handles	37.50	35.00	37.50	20.00	20.00
Bowl, 8" d, sq, two handles	38.00	40.00	38.00	20.00	20.00
Bowl, 9" d, scalloped, 1-3/4" deep, ftd	28.00	32.00	30.00	—	—
Bowl, 10" d, two handles, turned-up edge	30.00	34.00	32.00	—	—
Cake plate, 10-1/2" d, 1-1/4" h, ftd	45.00	47.00	40.00	—	—
Cake plate, 10-1/2" d, two handles	26.00	40.00	28.00	17.50	17.50
Candlesticks, pr, single lite	28.00	42.50	30.00	24.00	28.00
Candlesticks, pr, two lite	50.00	50.00	60.00	30.00	32.00
Creamer	21.00	20.00	22.50	20.00	24.00
Cup	15.00	15.00	14.00	12.50	12.50
Fruit bowl, 4-7/8" sq	16.00	20.00	18.00	12.00	12.50
Fruit bowl, 9-1/4" sq	30.00	50.00	35.00	20.00	20.00
Fruit bowl, 10" d, scalloped	40.00	40.00	40.00	—	—
Leaf, 8" l	12.50	17.50	16.00	—	—
Leaf, 11-1/4" l	25.00	30.00	28.00	—	—
Mayonnaise, 5-1/2" h, three ftd	25.00	30.00	35.00	17.50	17.50
Mint, 6" d, center handle	25.00	27.50	30.00	16.00	16.00
Plate, 7" h, two handles, scalloped	15.00	16.00	18.00	12.50	12.50
Plate, 8" d, scalloped	16.00	15.00	16.00	12.50	12.50
Plate, 8" d, scalloped, three ftd	17.50	27.00	17.50	12.50	12.50
Plate, 8" w, sq	17.50	25.00	17.50	12.50	12.50
Plate, 8-1/4" w, sq, indent for cup	17.50	19.00	17.50	—	—
Plate, 9" d, grill	20.00	20.00	20.00	—	—
Plate, 12" d, two handles	35.00	35.00	35.00	20.00	20.00
Rose bowl, 4" d	25.00	30.00	27.50	20.00	20.00
Salt and pepper shakers, pr	50.00	50.00	45.00	25.00	25.00
Sandwich server, center handle	40.00	37.50	40.00	—	—
Saucer	5.00	5.00	5.00	3.50	3.50
Sherbet	15.00	15.00	18.00	12.50	12.50
Sugar	9.00	22.50	22.00	20.00	20.00
Tumbler, ftd	25.00	27.50	32.50	—	—
Vase, 7-1/4" h	30.00	35.00	40.00	—	35.00

Mt. Pleasant, black creamer, **$20**; sugar (on pedestal), **$22.50**; scalloped bowl with two handles, **$35**; cup, **$15**.

Mt. Pleasant, black scalloped fruit bowl, **$40.**

National

Manufactured by Jeannette Glass Company, Jeannette, Pa., from the late 1940s to the mid-1950s.

Pieces are made in crystal, pink, and shell pink. Collector interest is primarily with crystal. Prices for pink and shell pink are not yet firmly established, but usually command slightly higher than crystal.

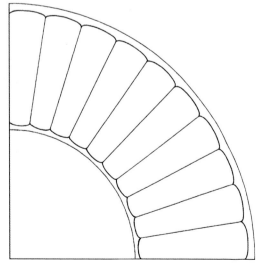

Item	Crystal		Item	Crystal
Ashtray	4.50		Punch bowl stand	10.00
Berry bowl, 4-1/2" d	4.00		Punch bowl, 12" d	25.00
Berry bowl, 8-1/2" d	8.00		Punch cup	3.50
Bowl, 12" d	15.00		Relish, three parts	15.00
Candleholders, pr	30.00		Salt and pepper shakers, pr	10.00
Candy dish, cov, ftd	20.00		Saucer	1.00
Cigarette box	15.00		Sherbet, 3-1/4" h, ftd	10.00
Creamer	5.00		Sugar, open	6.50
Creamer and sugar tray	6.00		Serving plate, 15" d	17.50
Cup	4.00		Tray, two handles	17.50
Jar, cov	15.00		Tumbler, ftd	8.50
Lazy Susan	40.00		Vase, 9"	20.00
Milk pitcher, 20 oz	20.00		Water pitcher, 64 oz	30.00
Plate, 8" d	6.50			

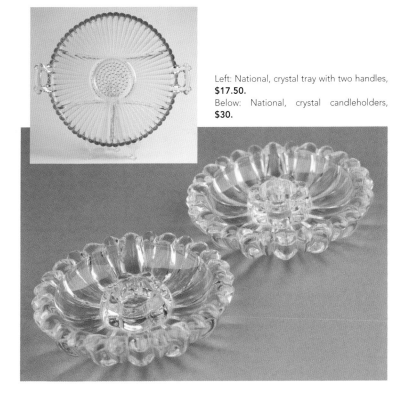

Left: National, crystal tray with two handles, **$17.50.**
Below: National, crystal candleholders, **$30.**

New Century

Manufactured by Hazel Atlas Company, Clarksburg, W.V., and Zanesville, Ohio, from 1930 to 1935.

Pieces are made in crystal and green, with limited production in amethyst, cobalt blue, and pink.

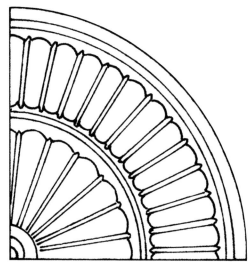

Item	Amethyst	Cobalt Blue	Crystal	Green	Pink
Ashtray/coaster, 5-3/8" d	—	—	30.00	30.00	—
Berry bowl, 4-1/2" d	—	—	35.00	35.00	—
Berry bowl, 8" d	—	—	30.00	30.00	—
Butter dish, cov	—	—	75.00	75.00	—
Casserole, cov, 9" d	—	—	115.00	115.00	—
Cocktail, 3-1/4 oz	—	—	42.00	42.00	
Cream soup, 4-3/4" d	—	—	25.00	25.00	—
Creamer			12.00	14.00	—
Cup	20.00	20.00	10.00	12.00	20.00
Decanter, stopper	—	—	90.00	90.00	—
Pitcher, with or without ice lip, 60 oz	55.00	55.00	45.00	48.00	50.00
Pitcher, with or without ice lip, 80 oz	55.00	55.00	45.00	48.00	50.00
Plate, 6" d, sherbet	—	—	6.00	6.50	—
Plate, 7-1/8" d, breakfast	—	—	12.00	12.00	
Plate, 8-1/2" d, salad	—	—	10.00	12.00	—
Plate, 10" d, dinner	—	—	24.00	24.00	—
Plate, 10" d, grill	—	—	15.00	18.00	—
Platter, 11" l, oval	—	—	30.00	30.00	—
Salt and pepper shakers, pr	—	—	45.00	45.00	—
Saucer	7.50	7.50	5.00	6.50	8.00
Sherbet, 3" h	—	—	9.00	9.00	—
Sugar, cov	—	—	40.00	45.00	—
Tumbler, 5 oz, 3-1/2" h	12.00	16.50	15.00	18.00	18.00
Tumbler, 5 oz, 4" h, ftd	—	—	30.00	32.50	—
Tumbler, 8 oz, 3-1/2" h	—	—	25.00	27.50	—
Tumbler, 9 oz, 4-1/4" h	15.00	20.00	24.00	18.00	15.00
Tumbler, 9 oz, 4-7/8" h, ftd	—	—	25.00	25.00	—
Tumbler, 10 oz, 5" h	16.00	30.00	20.00	17.50	16.00
Tumbler, 12 oz, 5-1/4" h	25.00	40.00	30.00	32.50	20.00
Whiskey, 2-1/2" h, 1-1/2 oz	—	—	18.00	20.00	—
Wine, 2-1/2 oz	—	—	35.00	40.00	—

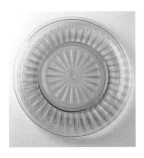

Far left: New Century, green dinner plate, **$24.**

Left: New Century, green salt and pepper shakers, **$45.**

Normandie
Bouquet and Lattice

Manufactured by Federal Glass Company, Columbus, Ohio, from 1933 to 1940.

Pieces are made in amber, crystal, iridescent, and pink.

Item	Amber	Crystal	Iridescent	Pink
Berry bowl, 5" d	9.50	6.00	7.50	14.00
Berry bowl, 8-1/2" d	35.00	24.00	30.00	80.00
Cereal bowl, 6-1/2" d	30.00	20.00	12.00	35.00
Creamer, ftd	20.00	10.00	10.00	15.00
Cup	7.50	4.00	10.00	12.50
Iced tea tumbler, 12 oz, 5" h	45.00	—	—	—
Juice tumbler, 5 oz, 4" h	40.00	—	—	—
Pitcher, 80 oz, 8" h	115.00	—	—	245.00
Plate, 6" d, sherbet	4.50	2.00	3.00	10.00
Plate, 7-3/4" d, salad	13.00	5.00	55.00	14.00
Plate, 9-1/4" d, luncheon	25.00	6.00	16.50	100.00
Plate, 11" d, dinner	55.00	15.00	12.00	18.00
Plate, 11" d, grill	15.00	8.00	8.00	25.00
Platter, 11-3/4" l	24.00	10.00	12.00	80.00
Salt and pepper shakers, pr	50.00	20.00	—	4.00
Saucer	4.00	1.50	2.50	10.00
Sherbet	7.50	6.00	7.50	9.50
Sugar	10.00	6.00	9.50	12.00
Tumbler, 9 oz, 4-1/4" h	25.00	10.00	—	50.00
Vegetable bowl, 10" l, oval	27.50	12.00	25.00	45.00

Above: Normandie, iridescent cup, **$10.**

Left: Normandie, iridescent dinner plate, **$12.**

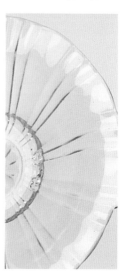

Old Café

Manufactured by Hocking Glass Company, Lancaster, Ohio, from 1936 to 1940.

Pieces are made in crystal, pink, and royal ruby.

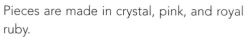

Old Café, royal ruby berry bowl, **$9.**

Item	Crystal	Pink	Royal Ruby
Berry bowl, 3-3/4" d	9.50	10.00	9.00
Bowl, 4-1/2" d, handle	—	18.00	—
Bowl, 6-1/2" d	15.00	18.00	—
Bowl, 9" d, closed handles	12.00	10.00	15.00
Candy dish, 8" d, low	12.50	18.50	20.00
Candy jar, 5-1/2" d, crystal with ruby cover	—	—	30.00
Cereal bowl, 5-1/2" d	30.00	30.00	30.00
Cup	12.00	16.00	12.00
Juice tumbler, 3" h	18.00	25.00	20.00
Lamp	100.00	100.00	150.00
Mint tray, 8" l	—	—	20.00
Olive dish, 6" l, oblong	7.50	10.00	—
Pitcher, 36 oz, 6" h	125.00	145.00	—
Pitcher, 80 oz	150.00	165.00	—
Plate, 6" d, sherbet	5.00	5.00	—
Plate, 10" d, dinner	60.00	65.00	—
Saucer	5.00	5.00	—
Sherbet, low, ftd	7.50	18.00	12.00
Tumbler, 4" h	18.00	20.00	18.00
Vase, 7-1/4" h	25.00	45.00	50.00

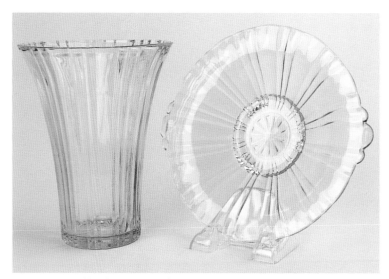

Old Café, crystal vase, **$25**; and bowl, 9-1/2" d, crystal, **$40.**

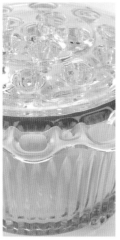

Old Colony
Lace Edge, Open Lace

Manufactured by Hocking Glass Company, Lancaster, Ohio, from 1935 to 1938.

Pieces are made in crystal and pink. Crystal Old Colony pieces are valued at about 50 percent of pink, as are frosted or satin finish prices. Many other companies made a look-alike to Old Colony, so care must be exercised. Some Old Colony plates have solid, flatter loops. Pieces hard to find are candlesticks, the 9-inch comport, tumblers and vase.

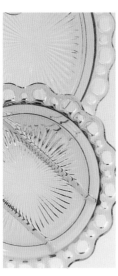

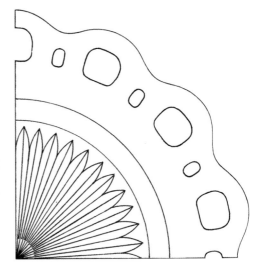

Item	Pink	Item	Pink
Bonbon, cov	65.00	Plate, 10-1/2" d, grill	28.50
Bowl, 9-1/2" d, plain	32.50	Plate, 13" d, four parts, solid lace	65.00
Bowl, 9-1/2" d, ribbed	35.00		
Butter dish, cov	100.00	Plate, 13" d, solid lace	65.00
Candlesticks, pr	350.00	Platter, 12-3/4" l	48.00
Candy jar, cov, ribbed	65.00	Platter, 12-3/4" l, five parts	42.00
Cereal bowl, 6-3/8" d	30.00	Relish, 7-1/2" d, three parts, deep	60.00
Comport, 7" d, cov	60.00		
Comport, 9" d	950.00	Relish, 10-1/2" d, three parts	35.00
Console bowl, 10-1/2" d, three legs	325.00	Relish, 13" l, divided	75.00
		Salad bowl, 7-3/4" d, ribbed	60.00
Cookie jar, cov	110.00	Saucer	12.00
Creamer	40.00	Sherbet, ftd	175.00
Cup	40.00	Sugar	25.00
Flower bowl, crystal frog	50.00	Tumbler, 5 oz, 3-1/2" h, flat	120.00
Plate, 7-1/4" d, salad	35.00	Tumbler, 9 oz, 4-1/2" h, flat	32.50
Plate, 8-1/4" d, luncheon	30.00	Tumbler, 10-1/2 oz, 5" h, ftd	95.00
Plate, 10-1/2" d, dinner	40.00	Vase, 7" h	650.00

Old Colony, pink platter, 12-3/4" l, divided, **$42.**

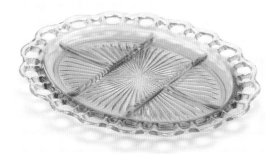

Old Colony, pink platter, 12-3/4" l, plain, **$48.**

Old Colony, pink satin-finish candlestick, **$350** for pair.

Old Colony, pink flower bowl with crystal frog, **$50.**

Old Colony, pink flower butter dish, covered, **$100.**

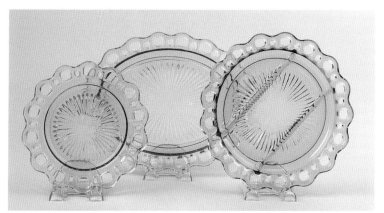

Old Colony, pink luncheon plate, **$30**; platter, **$48**; divided relish, **$35**.

Old Colony, pink bowl, 9-1/2" d, ribbed, **$35**.

Old Colony, pink bowl, 9-1/2" d, plain, **$32.50**.

Old English

Threading

Manufactured by Indiana Glass Company, Dunkirk, Ind., late 1920s.

Pieces are made in amber, crystal, green, and pink.

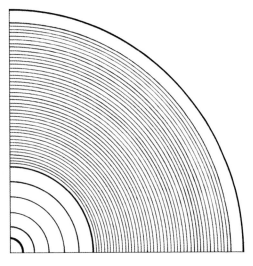

Item	Amber	Crystal	Green	Pink
Bowl, 4" d, flat	20.00	18.00	22.00	20.00
Bowl, 9-1/2" d, flat	35.00	25.00	35.00	35.00
Candlesticks, pr, 4" h	35.00	25.00	45.00	35.00
Candy dish, cov, flat	50.00	40.00	50.00	50.00
Candy jar, cov	55.00	45.00	55.00	55.00
Cheese compote, 3-1/2" h	17.50	12.00	17.50	17.50
Cheese plate, indent	20.00	10.00	20.00	20.00
Compote, 3-1/2" h, 6-3/8" w, two handles	24.00	12.00	24.00	24.00
Compote, 3-1/2" h, 7" w	24.00	12.00	24.00	24.00
Creamer	18.00	10.00	18.00	18.00
Eggcup	—	10.00	—	—
Fruit bowl, 9" d, ftd	30.00	20.00	30.00	30.00
Fruit stand, 11" h, ftd	50.00	18.00	40.00	40.00
Goblet, 8 oz, 5-3/4" h	30.00	15.00	30.00	30.00
Pitcher	70.00	35.00	70.00	70.00
Pitcher, cov	125.00	55.00	125.00	125.00
Sandwich server, center handle	60.00	—	60.00	60.00
Sherbet	20.00	10.00	20.00	20.00
Sugar, cov	38.00	14.00	38.00	38.00
Tumbler, 4-1/2" h, ftd	24.00	12.00	32.50	28.00
Tumbler, 5-1/2" h, ftd	40.00	20.00	40.00	65.00
Vase, 5-3/8" h, 7" w, fan-shape	48.00	24.00	48.00	48.00
Vase, 8" h, 4-1/2" w, ftd	45.00	20.00	45.00	45.00
Vase, 8-1/4" h, 4-1/4" w, ftd	45.00	20.00	45.00	45.00
Vase, 12" h, ftd	72.00	35.00	72.00	72.00

Old English, green compote, **$24.**

Ovide

Manufactured by Hazel Atlas Glass Company, Clarksburg, W.V., and Zanesville, Ohio, 1930-35 and in the 1950s.

Pieces are made in black, green, and white Platonite with fired-on colors in the 1950s.

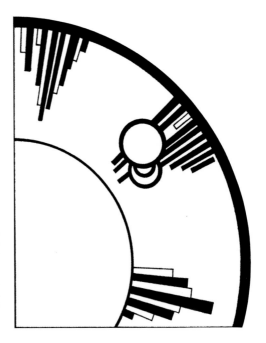

Item	Black	Green	Platonite
Berry bowl, 4-3/4" d	—	5.50	6.00
Berry bowl, 8" d	—	—	22.00
Bowl, 6" d	—	—	9.00
Candy dish, cov	50.00	24.00	35.00
Cereal bowl, 5-1/2" d	10.00	—	12.50
Creamer	10.00	6.00	18.00
Cup	8.00	4.50	5.00
Eggcup	—	—	22.00
Fruit cocktail, ftd	5.00	4.50	—
Plate, 6" d, sherbet	—	2.50	6.00
Plate, 7" d, salad	—	4.50	4.50
Plate, 8" d, luncheon	8.00	3.50	15.00
Plate, 9" d, dinner	—	8.00	10.00
Platter, 11" d	—	—	24.00
Salt and pepper shakers, pr	32.00	28.00	25.00
Saucer	4.50	2.50	3.00
Sherbet	6.50	3.50	5.00
Soup bowl, 8" d	—	20.00	20.00
Sugar, open	10.00	7.00	20.00
Tumbler	18.00	—	14.00
Vase, 6" h, sterling silver trim	35.00	—	—

Ovide, pink and gray platonite luncheon plate, **$15.**

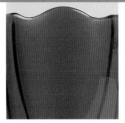

Oyster and Pearl

Manufactured by Anchor Hocking Glass Corporation, from 1938 to 1940.

Pieces are made in crystal, pink, royal ruby, and white with fired-on green or pink.

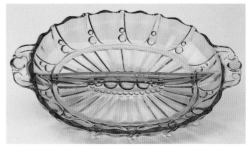

Oyster and Pearl, pink relish dish, **$35.**

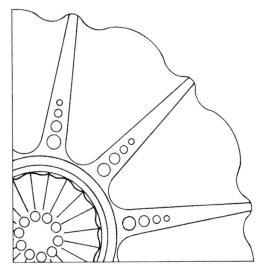

Item	Crystal	Pink	Royal Ruby	White, Fired-On Green	White, Fired-On Pink
Bowl, 5-1/2" d, handle	8.00	15.00	20.00	—	—
Bowl, 5-1/4" w, handle, heart-shape	15.00	21.00	—	20.00	15.00
Bowl, 6-1/2" d, handle	12.00	15.00	28.00	—	—
Candle holders, pr, 3-1/2" h	35.00	45.00	65.00	25.00	25.00
Fruit bowl, 10-1/2" d, deep	20.00	25.00	50.00	30.00	30.00
Relish dish, 10-1/4" l, divided	10.00	35.00	—	—	—
Sandwich plate, 13-1/2" d	20.00	40.00	50.00	—	—

Left: Oyster and Pearl, royal ruby sandwich plate, **$50.**

Below: Oyster and Pearl, royal ruby bowl with handles, **$20.**

Parrot
Sylvan

Manufactured by Federal Glass Company, Columbus, Ohio, from 1931 to 1932.

Pieces are made in amber and green, with limited production in blue and crystal.

Item	Amber	Green
Berry bowl, 5" d	22.50	30.00
Berry bowl, 8" d	75.00	80.00
Butter dish, cov	1,250.00	475.00
Creamer, ftd	65.00	55.00
Cup	35.00	40.00
Fruit bowl	—	40.00
Hot plate, 5" d, pointed	875.00	900.00
Hot plate, round	—	950.00
Jam dish, 7" d	35.00	—
Pitcher, 80 oz, 8-1/2" h	—	2,500.00
Plate, 5-3/4" d, sherbet	45.00	35.00
Plate, 7-1/2" d, salad	—	60.00
Plate, 9" d, dinner	50.00	95.00
Plate, 10-1/2" d, grill, round	35.00	—
Plate, 10-1/2" d, grill, square	—	60.00
Platter, 11-1/4" l, oblong	65.00	70.00
Salt and pepper shakers, pr	—	270.00
Saucer	18.00	18.00
Sherbet, ftd, cone	22.50	27.50
Soup bowl, 7" d	35.00	60.00
Sugar, cov	450.00	320.00
Tumbler, 10 oz, 4-1/4" h	100.00	130.00
Tumbler, 10 oz, 5-1/2" h, ftd, Madrid mold	145.00	—
Tumbler, 12 oz, 5-1/2" h	115.00	160.00
Tumbler, 5-3/4" h, ftd, heavy	100.00	120.00
Vegetable bowl, 10" l, oval	75.00	65.00

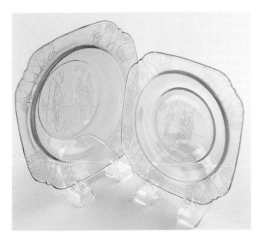

Parrot, amber jam dish, **$35**; green sherbet plate, **$35.**

P

Patrician
Spoke

Manufactured by Federal Glass Company, Columbus, Ohio, from 1933 to 1937.

Pieces are made in amber (also called Golden Glo), crystal, green, and pink.

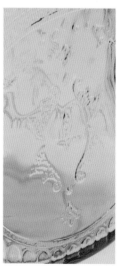

Item	Amber	Crystal	Green	Pink
Berry bowl, 5" d	12.50	10.00	12.50	18.50
Berry bowl, 8-1/2" d	35.00	15.00	37.50	35.00
Butter dish, cov	100.00	100.00	215.00	225.00
Cereal bowl, 6" d	30.00	27.50	27.50	25.00
Cookie jar, cov	75.00	80.00	500.00	—
Cream soup, 4-3/4" d	20.00	25.00	24.50	22.00
Creamer, ftd	12.50	9.50	12.50	12.50
Cup	10.00	12.00	15.00	18.50
Iced tea tumbler, 14 oz, 5-1/2" h	45.00	40.00	42.00	45.00
Jam dish	30.00	25.00	35.00	30.00
Mayonnaise, three toes	—	—	—	165.00
Pitcher, 75 oz, 8" h, molded handle	120.00	125.00	125.00	115.00
Pitcher, 75 oz, 8-1/4" h, applied handle	150.00	140.00	150.00	145.00
Plate, 6" d, sherbet	10.00	8.50	10.00	10.00
Plate, 7-1/2" d, salad	18.00	15.00	20.00	15.00
Plate, 9" d, luncheon	15.00	12.50	12.00	22.50
Plate, 10-1/2" d, grill	15.00	13.50	20.00	20.00
Plate, 10-1/2" d, dinner	12.50	12.75	32.00	36.00
Platter, 11-1/2" l, oval	35.00	30.00	30.00	28.00
Salt and pepper shakers, pr	65.00	65.00	65.00	85.00
Saucer	10.00	9.25	9.50	12.50
Sherbet	14.00	12.00	14.00	16.00
Sugar	12.50	9.00	18.50	12.50
Sugar lid	55.00	50.00	75.00	60.00
Tumbler, 5 oz, 4" h	40.00	28.50	30.00	32.00
Tumbler, 8 oz, 5-1/4" h, ftd	50.00	42.00	50.00	—
Tumbler, 9 oz, 4-1/4" h	32.00	28.50	25.00	28.00
Tumbler, 12 oz	45.00	—	—	—
Vegetable bowl, 10" l, oval	35.00	30.00	38.50	30.00

Patrician, amber sherbet, **$14**; cream soup, **$20.**

Patrician, amber salt and pepper shakers, **$65.**

Patrician, amber pitcher, molded handle, 8" h, 75 oz, **$120.**

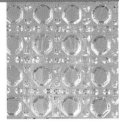

Patrick

Manufactured by Lancaster Glass Company, Lancaster, Ohio, early 1930s.

Pieces are made in pink and yellow.

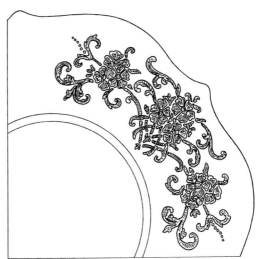

P

Patrick

Item	Pink	Yellow
Candlesticks, pr	200.00	160.00
Candy dish, three ftd	175.00	175.00
Cheese and cracker set	150.00	130.00
Cocktail, 4" h	85.00	85.00
Console bowl, 11" d	150.00	150.00
Creamer	90.00	40.00
Cup	85.00	40.00
Fruit bowl, 9" d, handle	175.00	130.00
Goblet, 10 oz, 6" h	85.00	75.00
Juice goblet, 6 oz, 4-3/4" h	85.00	75.00
Mayonnaise, three pieces	200.00	140.00
Plate, 7" d, sherbet	20.00	15.00
Plate, 7-1/2" d, salad	25.00	20.00
Plate, 8" d, luncheon	45.00	30.00
Plate, 9" d	60.00	—
Saucer	20.00	12.00
Sherbet, 4-3/4" d	72.00	60.00
Sugar	90.00	40.00
Tray, 11" d, center handle	165.00	120.00
Tray, 11" d, two handles	80.00	65.00

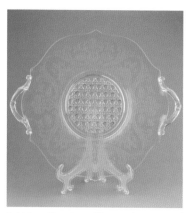

Patrick, yellow tray with caned center and two handles, **$65.**

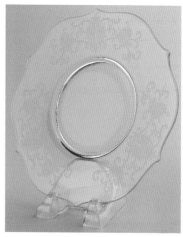

Patrick, yellow luncheon plate, **$30.**

Petalware

Manufactured by Macbeth-Evans Glass Company, Charleroi, Pa., from 1930 to 1940.

Made in cobalt blue, Cremax, crystal, fired-on red, blue, green and yellow, Monax and pink. Florette is the name given to a floral decorated with a pointed petal. There are other patterns, such as red flowers with a red rim, fruit and other floral patterns.

Crystal values are approximately 50 percent less than those listed for Cremax. Cobalt blue production was limited and the mustard is currently valued at $15 when complete with its metal lid. Monax Regency is priced the same as Monax Florette.

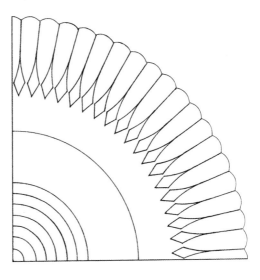

Item	Cremax	Cremax, Gold Trim	Fired-On Colors	Monax, Florette	Monax, Plain	Pink
Berry bowl, 9" d	30.00	32.00	—	35.50	18.00	25.00
Cereal bowl, 5-1/4" d	15.00	17.50	8.50	15.50	9.00	15.00
Cream soup liner	—	—	—	—	18.75	—
Cream soup, 4-1/2" d	12.50	12.00	12.00	15.00	10.00	19.00
Creamer, ftd	12.50	15.00	8.50	15.00	12.00	15.00
Cup	8.00	10.00	9.50	12.00	6.50	6.00
Lamp shade, 9" d	16.50	—	—	14.00	18.00	—
Plate, 6" d, sherbet	4.50	50.00	6.00	6.00	2.50	4.50
Plate, 8" d, salad	12.00	8.00	7.50	15.00	4.50	10.00
Plate, 9" d, dinner	25.00	14.00	8.50	16.50	9.00	20.00
Platter, 13" l, oval	25.00	20.00	20.00	25.00	20.00	17.50
Salver, 11" d	15.00	17.00	14.00	25.00	15.00	17.50
Salver, 12" d	—	—	—	—	24.00	22.50
Saucer	3.50	3.00	4.00	5.00	3.50	5.00
Sherbet, 4" h, low ftd	—	—	—	—	32.00	—
Sherbet, 4-1/2" h, low ftd	15.00	12.00	8.00	12.00	10.00	8.50
Soup bowl, 7" d	65.00	60.00	70.00	65.00	60.00	—
Sugar, ftd	7.50	11.00	12.00	15.00	10.00	9.00
Tumbler, 12 oz, 4-5/8" h	—	—	—	—	—	25.00

Petalware, pink sugar, **$9**, and creamer, **$15**; two dinner plates, **$20 each**.

Petalware, Cremax sugar with gold rim, **$11**; Cremax cream, **$12.50.**

Petalware, Monax lampshade with flower decoration, **$14.**

Petalware, Monax dinner plate, **$9.**

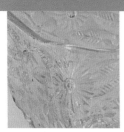

Pineapple and Floral

No. 618

Manufactured by Indiana Glass Company, Dunkirk, Ind., from 1932 to 1937.

Pieces are made in amber, avocado (late 1960s), cobalt blue (1980s), crystal, fired-on green, fired-on red, and pink (1980s).

Reproductions: † A salad bowl and diamond-shaped comport have been reproduced in several different colors, including crystal, pink, and avocado green.

Item	Amber	Crystal	Red
Ashtray, 4-1/2" d	20.00	16.50	20.00
Berry bowl, 4-3/4" d	24.00	20.00	22.00
Cereal bowl, 6" d	24.00	30.00	22.00
Comport, diamond-shape	10.00	3.50	10.00
Creamer, diamond-shape	10.00	9.50	10.00
Cream soup	16.50	18.00	16.50
Cup	10.00	12.00	10.00
Plate, 6" d, sherbet	8.00	7.50	8.00
Plate, 8-3/8" d, salad	12.00	8.00	12.00
Plate, 9-3/8" d, dinner	17.50	18.00	17.50
Plate, 9-3/4" d, indentation	—	25.00	—
Plate, 11" d, closed handles	24.00	20.00	24.00
Plate, 11-1/2" d, indentation	—	25.00	—
Platter, 11" l, closed handles	20.00	8.00	20.00
Relish, 11-1/2" d, divided	28.00	20.00	28.00
Salad bowl, 7" d †	10.00	5.00	10.00
Sandwich plate, 11-1/2" d	24.00	20.00	24.00
Saucer	4.50	5.00	7.50
Sherbet, ftd	28.00	24.00	28.00
Sugar, diamond-shape	10.00	9.50	10.00
Tumbler, 8 oz, 4-1/4" h	40.00	40.00	40.00
Tumbler, 12 oz, 5" h	48.00	46.50	48.00
Vase, cone shape	45.00	42.50	45.00
Vegetable bowl, 10" l, oval	32.00	30.00	32.00

Pineapple and Floral, amber cream soup bowl, **$16.50.**

Pineapple and Floral, crystal footed sherbet, **$24.**

P

Pioneer

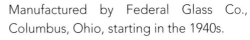

Manufactured by Federal Glass Co., Columbus, Ohio, starting in the 1940s.

Pieces were originally made in pink; crystal was added later. The crystal 11-inch fluted bowl and a 12-inch dinner plate were made until 1973.

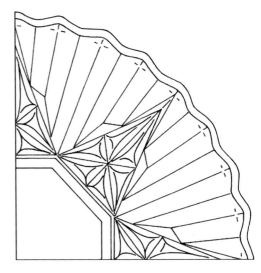

Item	Crystal	Pink
Bowl, 7" d, low, fruits center	8.00	10.00
Bowl, 7-3/4" d, ruffled, fruits center	10.00	12.00
Bowl, 10-1/2" d, fruits center	12.00	14.00
Bowl, 10-1/2" d, plain center	10.00	12.00
Bowl, 11" d, ruffled, fruits center	15.00	18.00
Bowl, 11" d, ruffled, plain center	12.00	15.00
Nappy, 5-3/8" d, fruits center	8.00	10.00
Nappy, 5-3/8" d, plain center	6.00	8.00
Plate, 8" d, luncheon, fruits center	6.00	8.00
Plate, 8" d, luncheon, plain center	6.00	8.00
Plate, 12" d, fruits center	10.00	12.00
Plate, 12" d, plain center	10.00	12.00

Pioneer, pink luncheon plate, fruit center, **$8.**

Princess

Manufactured by Hocking Glass Company, Lancaster, Ohio, from 1931 to 1935.

Pieces are made in apricot yellow, blue, green, pink, and topaz yellow.

Reproductions: † The candy dish and salt and pepper shakers have been reproduced in blue, green and pink.

Item	Apricot Yellow	Blue	Green	Pink	Topaz Yellow
Ashtray, 4-1/2" d	110.00	—	72.00	90.00	110.00
Berry bowl, 4-1/2" d	55.00	—	40.00	30.00	55.00
Butter dish, cov	700.00	—	115.00	120.00	700.00
Cake plate, 10" d, ftd	—	—	40.00	100.00	—
Candy dish, cov †	—	—	75.00	95.00	—
Cereal bowl, 5" d	—	—	50.00	45.00	—
Coaster	100.00	—	85.00	65.00	100.00
Cookie jar, cov	—	875.00	85.00	75.00	—
Creamer, oval	25.00	—	15.00	17.50	22.50
Cup	10.00	120.00	15.00	17.50	15.00
Hat-shaped bowl, 9-1/2" d	125.00	—	80.00	50.00	125.00
Iced tea tumbler, 13 oz, 5-1/2" h	45.00	—	125.00	115.00	30.00
Juice tumbler, 5 oz, 3" h	28.00	—	25.00	28.00	30.00
Pitcher, 24 oz, 7-3/8" h, ftd	—	—	550.00	475.00	—
Pitcher, 37 oz, 6" h	775.00	—	60.00	75.00	775.00
Pitcher, 60 oz, 8" h	95.00	—	65.00	80.00	95.00
Plate, 5-1/2" d, sherbet	4.75	65.00	15.00	12.00	4.75
Plate, 8" d, salad	15.00	—	20.00	15.00	20.00
Plate, 9-1/2" d, dinner	25.00	—	30.00	35.00	30.00
Plate, 9-1/2" d, grill	10.00	175.00	20.00	15.00	10.00
Plate, 10-1/2" d, grill, closed handles	10.00	—	15.00	15.00	10.00
Platter, 12" l, closed handles	60.00	—	25.00	25.00	60.00
Relish, 7-1/2" l, divided, four parts	100.00	—	35.00	30.00	100.00
Relish, 7-1/2" l, plain	225.00	—	195.00	195.00	225.00
Salad bowl, 9" d, octagonal	125.00	—	55.00	40.00	125.00
Salt and pepper shakers, pr, 4-1/2" h †	75.00	—	60.00	65.00	85.00
Sandwich plate, 10-1/4" d, two closed handles	175.00	—	30.00	35.00	175.00
Saucer, 6" sq	2.75	65.00	14.50	10.00	3.75
Sherbet, ftd	40.00	—	25.00	25.00	40.00
Spice shakers, pr, 5-1/2" h	—	—	20.00	—	—
Sugar, cov	30.00	—	35.00	65.00	30.00
Tumbler, 9 oz, 4" h	25.00	—	28.00	25.00	25.00
Tumbler, 9 oz, 4-3/4" h, sq, ftd	—	—	65.00	25.00	—
Tumbler, 10 oz, 5-1/4" h, ftd	18.00	—	35.00	35.00	30.00
Tumbler, 12-1/2 oz, 6-1/2" h, ftd	25.00	—	180.00	95.00	25.00
Vase, 8" h	—	—	65.00	75.00	—
Vegetable bowl, 10" l, oval	60.00	—	50.00	50.00	65.00

Princess, green salad bowl, octagonal, **$55.**

Princess, green cookie jar, **$85.**

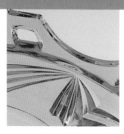

Pyramid
No. 610

Manufactured by Indiana Glass Company, Dunkirk, Ind., from 1926 to 1932.

Made in crystal, green, pink, white, and yellow. Later production in 1974 to 1975 by Tiara produced black and blue pieces. Production limited in blue and white. Prices for black are not firmly established in the secondary market at this time.

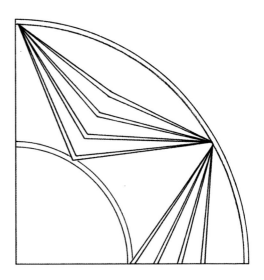

Item	Black	Crystal	Green	Pink	Yellow
Berry bowl, 4-3/4" d	15.00	20.00	35.00	35.00	65.00
Berry bowl, 8-1/2" d	40.00	30.00	65.00	55.00	75.00
Bowl, 9-1/2" l, oval	—	50.00	45.00	40.00	65.00
Creamer	50.00	20.00	35.00	35.00	40.00
Ice tub	—	95.00	145.00	155.00	225.00
Pickle dish, 9-1/2" l, 5-3/4" w	—	30.00	35.00	35.00	65.00
Pitcher	—	395.00	265.00	400.00	550.00
Relish, four parts, handles	27.50	25.00	65.00	60.00	70.00
Sugar	50.00	20.00	35.00	35.00	40.00
Tray for creamer and sugar	85.00	25.00	30.00	30.00	35.00
Tumbler, 8 oz, ftd	—	55.00	50.00	55.00	75.00
Tumbler, 11 oz, ftd	35.00	70.00	75.00	50.00	95.00

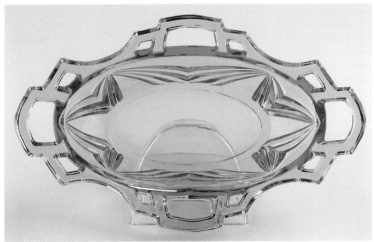

Pyramid, green pickle dish, **$35.**

Queen Mary
Prismatic Line, Vertical Ribbed

Manufactured by Hocking Glass Company, Lancaster, Ohio, from 1936 to 1948.

Pieces are made in crystal, pink, and royal ruby.

Queen Mary, crystal bowl, 7" d, **$7.50**; candlesticks, pair, **$30.**

Item	Crystal	Pink	Royal Ruby
Ashtray, 2" x 3-3/4" l, oval	5.00	5.50	5.00
Ashtray, 3-1/2" d, round	4.00	—	—
Berry bowl, 4-1/2" d	3.00	8.00	—
Berry bowl, 5" d	5.00	15.00	—
Berry bowl, 8-3/4" d	10.00	17.50	—
Bowl, 4" d, one handle	4.00	7.50	—
Bowl, 5-1/2" d, two handles	8.00	15.00	—
Bowl, 7" d	7.50	35.00	—
Bowl, 7-1/2" d, rimmed	—	40.00	—
Butter dish, cov	42.00	125.00	—
Candlesticks, pr, two lite, 4-1/2" h	30.00	—	70.00
Candy dish, cov	70.00	42.00	—
Celery tray, 5" x 10"	10.00	24.00	—
Cereal bowl, 6" d	8.00	30.00	—
Cigarette jar, 2" x 3" oval	6.50	7.50	—
Coaster, 3-1/2" d	4.00	5.00	—
Coaster/ashtray, 4-1/4" sq	4.00	6.00	—
Comport, 5-3/4"	9.00	14.00	—
Creamer, ftd	8.00	40.00	—
Creamer, oval	8.00	12.00	—
Cup, large	6.00	9.50	—
Cup, small	8.00	12.00	—
Custard cup	—	22.00	—
Juice tumbler, 5 oz, 3-1/2" h	9.50	18.00	—
Pickle dish, 5" x 10"	10.00	24.00	—
Plate, 6" d, sherbet	4.00	10.00	—
Plate, 6-1/2" d, bread and butter	6.00	—	—
Plate, 8-1/4" d, salad	6.00	—	—
Plate, 9-1/2" d, dinner	35.00	65.00	—
Preserve, cov	30.00	125.00	—
Relish, clover-shape	15.00	17.50	—
Relish, 12" d, three parts	10.00	15.00	—
Relish, 14" d, four parts	15.00	17.50	—
Salt and pepper shakers, pr	30.00	—	—
Sandwich plate, 12" d	20.00	17.50	—
Saucer	2.00	5.00	—
Serving tray, 14" d	15.00	9.00	—
Sherbet, ftd	6.00	15.00	—
Sugar, ftd	—	40.00	—
Sugar, oval	8.00	24.00	—
Tumbler, 9 oz, 4" h	6.00	17.50	—
Tumbler, 10 oz, 5" h, ftd	35.00	70.00	—

Radiance

Manufactured by New Martinsville Glass Company, New Martinsville, W.V., from 1936 to 1939.

Pieces are made in amber, cobalt blue, crystal, emerald green, ice blue, pink, and red. Some pieces are found with an etched design, which adds slightly to the value.

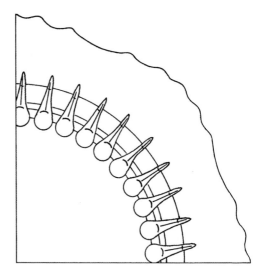

Item	Amber	Cobalt Blue	Crystal	Emerald Green	Ice Blue	Pink	Red
Bonbon, 6" d	16.00	—	8.00	—	32.00	—	32.00
Bonbon, 6" d, cov	48.00	—	24.00	—	95.00	—	95.00
Bonbon, 6" d, ftd	18.00	—	9.00	—	35.00	—	35.00
Bowl, 6" d, ruffled	—	—	—	—	35.00	—	—
Bowl, 6-1/2" d, ftd, metal holder	—	—	—	—	—	—	32.00
Bowl, 10" d, crimped	28.00	—	14.00	—	48.00	—	48.00
Bowl, 10" d, flared	22.00	—	11.00	—	48.00	—	48.00
Bowl, 12" d, crimped	30.00	—	15.00	—	50.00	—	50.00
Bowl, 12" d, flared	28.00	—	14.00	—	50.00	—	50.00
Butter dish, cov	210.00	—	120.00	—	460.00	—	460.00
Butter dish, chrome lid	40.00	—	50.00	—	—	—	—
Cake salver	—	—	—	—	175.00	—	175.00
Candlesticks, pr, two lite	75.00	—	37.50	—	120.00	—	120.00

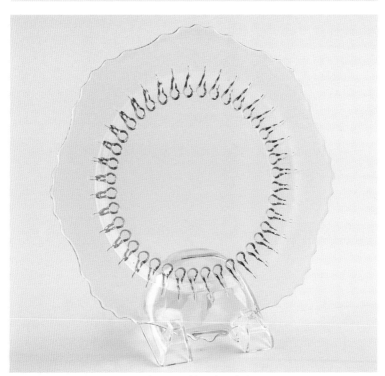

Radiance, ice blue plate, **$12.**

Item	Amber	Cobalt Blue	Crystal	Emerald Green	Ice Blue	Pink	Red
Candlesticks, pr, 6" h, ruffled	85.00	—	40.00	—	175.00	—	175.00
Candlesticks, pr, 8" h	60.00	—	30.00	—	110.00	—	110.00
Candy dish, cov, three parts	—	125.00	—	—	125.00	—	125.00
Celery tray, 10" l	18.00	—	9.00	—	32.00	—	32.00
Cheese and cracker set, 11" d plate	45.00	—	20.00	—	195.00	—	65.00
Comport, 5" h	18.00	—	9.00	—	30.00	—	30.00
Comport, 6" h	24.00	—	12.00	—	35.00	—	35.00
Condiment set, four pcs, tray	160.00	—	85.00	—	295.00	—	295.00
Cordial, 1 oz	30.00	55.00	15.00	—	45.00	—	45.00
Creamer	15.00	25.00	20.00	—	35.00	32.00	30.00
Cruet, individual	40.00	—	20.00	—	26.00	—	27.50
Cup, ftd	15.00	18.00	8.00	—	18.00	20.00	20.00
Decanter, stopper, handle	90.00	195.00	45.00	—	225.00	—	225.00
Lamp, 12" h	60.00	—	30.00	—	115.00	—	115.00
Mayonnaise, three-pc set	37.50	—	19.00	—	85.00	—	85.00
Nut bowl, 5" d, two handles	12.00	—	6.50	—	20.00	—	24.00
Pickle, 7" d	16.00	—	8.00	—	25.00	—	27.50
Pitcher, 64 oz	185.00	350.00	95.00	—	375.00	—	375.00
Pitcher, silver overlay	—	—	—	—	—	—	125.00
Plate, 8" d, luncheon	10.00	—	5.00	—	12.00	—	25.00
Punch bowl, 9" d	110.00	—	65.00	135.00	185.00	—	185.00
Punch bowl liner, 14" d	48.00	—	24.00	35.00	85.00	—	85.00
Punch cup	8.00	—	5.00	—	20.00	—	15.00
Punch ladle	100.00	—	45.00	—	120.00	—	120.00
Relish, 7" d, two parts	18.00	—	9.00	—	32.00	—	32.00
Relish, 8" d, three parts	28.00	—	15.00	—	35.00	—	35.00
Salt and pepper shakers, pr	50.00	—	25.00	—	90.00	95.00	95.00
Saucer	6.00	7.50	3.50	—	7.50	8.00	8.00
Sugar	16.00	—	20.00	—	30.00	32.00	30.00
Tray, oval	25.00	—	15.00	—	32.00	32.00	32.00
Tumbler, 9" oz	22.50	35.00	12.00	—	30.00	—	35.00
Vase, 10" h, crimped	48.00	75.00	24.00	—	60.00	—	70.00
Vase, 10" h, flared	48.00	75.00	24.00	—	60.00	—	70.00
Vase, 12" h, crimped	60.00	50.00	30.00	—	55.00	—	85.00
Vase, 12" h, flared	70.00	—	50.00	—	175.00	—	175.00

Raindrops
Optic Design

Manufactured by Federal Glass Company, Columbus, Ohio, from 1929 to 1933.

Pieces are made in crystal and green.

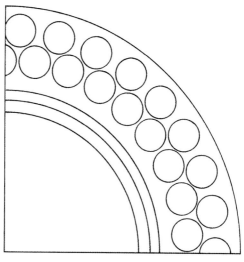

Item	Crystal	Green
Berry bowl, 7-1/2" d	30.00	45.00
Cereal bowl, 6" d	10.00	15.00
Creamer	8.00	10.00
Cup	8.50	8.50
Fruit bowl, 4-1/2" d	5.00	12.00
Plate, 6" d, sherbet	1.50	3.00
Plate, 8" d, luncheon	4.00	7.50
Salt and pepper shakers, pr	200.00	350.00
Saucer	3.00	4.50
Sherbet	4.50	7.50
Sugar, cov	7.50	15.00
Tumbler, 2 oz, 2-1/8" h	4.00	7.00
Tumbler, 4 oz, 3" h	4.00	7.00
Tumbler, 5 oz, 3-7/8" h	5.50	9.50
Tumbler, 9-1/2 oz, 4-1/8" h	6.00	12.00
Tumblers, 10 oz, 5" h	6.00	12.00
Tumblers, 14 oz, 5-3/8" h	7.50	15.00
Whiskey, 1 oz, 1-7/8" h	7.50	10.00

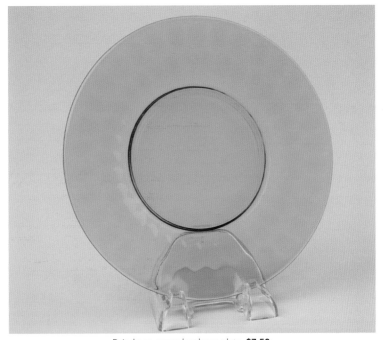

Raindrops, green luncheon plate, **$7.50.**

Ribbon

Manufactured by Hazel Atlas Glass Company, Clarksburg, W.V. and Zanesville, Ohio, early 1930s.

Pieces are made in black, crystal, green, and pink. Production in pink was limited to salt and pepper shakers, valued at $40.

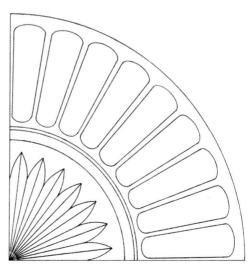

Item	Black	Crystal	Green
Berry bowl, 4" d	—	20.00	22.00
Berry bowl, 8" d	—	27.50	45.00
Bowl, 9" d, wide bands	—	—	35.00
Candy dish, cov	45.00	35.00	45.00
Cereal bowl, 5" d	—	20.00	25.00
Creamer, ftd	—	10.00	18.00
Cup	—	4.50	6.50
Plate, 6-1/4" d, sherbet	—	3.50	4.50
Plate, 8" d, luncheon	15.00	7.00	10.00
Salt and pepper shakers, pr	45.00	36.00	32.00
Saucer	—	2.00	3.50
Sherbet	—	6.00	8.00
Sugar, ftd	—	12.00	18.50
Tumbler, 10 oz, 6" h	—	28.00	30.00

Ribbon, green cup, **$6.50**; creamer, **$18.**

Ring
Banded Rings

Manufactured by Hocking Glass Company, Lancaster, Ohio, from 1927 to 1933.

Pieces are made in crystal, crystal with rings of black, blue, pink, red, orange, silver and yellow; and green, Mayfair blue, pink and red. Prices for decorated pieces are quite similar to each other.

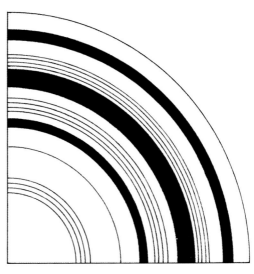

Item	Crystal	Decorated	Green
Berry bowl, 5" d	4.00	9.00	6.00
Berry bowl, 8" d	7.50	16.00	16.00
Bowl, 5-1/4" d, divided	12.50	—	—
Butter tub	24.00	25.00	20.00
Cereal bowl	—	5.00	8.00
Cocktail shaker	20.00	30.00	27.50
Cocktail, 3-1/2 oz, 3-3/4" h	12.00	18.00	18.00
Creamer, ftd	5.00	10.00	10.00
Cup	5.00	6.00	5.00
Decanter, stopper	30.00	35.00	32.00
Goblet, 9 oz, 7-1/4" h	7.00	15.00	14.00
Ice bucket	24.00	33.00	30.00
Ice tub	24.00	25.00	20.00
Iced tea tumbler, 6-1/2" h	10.00	15.00	15.00
Juice tumbler, 3-1/2" h, ftd	6.50	10.00	15.00
Old fashioned tumbler, 8 oz, 4" h	15.00	17.50	17.50
Pitcher, 60 oz, 8" h	15.00	25.00	25.00
Pitcher, 80 oz, 8-1/2" h	20.00	35.00	36.00
Plate, 6-1/2" d, off-center ring	5.50	6.50	8.00
Plate, 6-1/4" d, sherbet	3.25	6.50	4.00
Plate, 8" d, luncheon	3.00	6.00	9.00
Salt and pepper shakers, pr, 3" h	20.00	40.00	42.00
Sandwich plate, 11-3/4" d	9.50	15.00	15.00
Sandwich server, center handle	15.00	27.50	27.50
Saucer	1.50	4.00	2.50
Sherbet, 4-3/4" h	6.50	10.00	12.00
Sherbet, flat, 6-1/2" d underplate	12.00	18.00	21.00
Soup bowl, 7" d	10.00	9.00	8.00
Sugar, ftd	5.00	10.00	3.00
Tumbler, 4 oz, 3" h	4.00	6.50	6.00
Tumbler, 5-1/2" h, ftd	6.00	10.00	10.00
Tumbler, 5 oz, 3-1/2" h	5.00	6.50	12.00
Tumbler, 9 oz, 4-1/4" h	4.50	18.00	9.00
Tumbler, 10 oz, 4-3/4" h	8.50	—	9.00
Tumbler, 12 oz, 5-1/8" h, ftd	10.00	12.00	20.00
Vase, 8" h	20.00	35.00	37.50
Whiskey, 1-1/2 oz, 2" h	8.50	10.00	12.00
Wine, 3-1/2 oz, 4-1/2" h	17.50	20.00	24.00

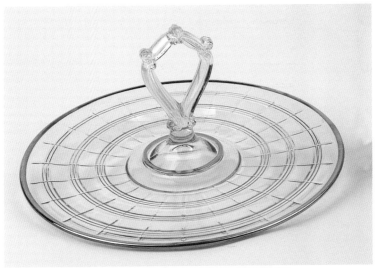

Ring, crystal sandwich server with center handle, **$15.**

Ring, green ice tub, **$20.**

Rose Cameo

Manufactured by Belmont Tumbler Company, Bellaire, Ohio, in 1931.

Pieces are made in green.

Item	Green
Berry bowl, 4-1/2" d	15.00
Cereal bowl, 5" d	27.50
Bowl, 6" d, straight sides	30.00
Plate, 7" d, salad	16.00
Sherbet	15.00
Tumbler, 5" h, ftd	25.00
Tumbler, 5" h, ftd, sterling silver trim	30.00

Rose Cameo, green tumbler, **$25.**

Rosemary
Dutch Rose

Manufactured by Federal Glass Company, Columbus, Ohio, from 1935 to 1937.

Pieces are made in amber, green, and pink.

Item	Amber	Green	Pink
Berry bowl, 5" d	7.00	17.50	17.50
Cereal bowl, 6" d	30.00	32.00	35.00
Cream soup, 5" d	20.00	25.00	30.00
Creamer, ftd	15.00	16.00	20.00
Cup	7.50	12.50	15.00
Plate, 6-3/4" d, salad	6.25	12.00	12.50
Plate, 9-1/2" d, dinner	10.00	15.00	30.00
Plate, 9-1/2" d, grill	12.00	15.00	22.00
Platter, 12" l, oval	18.00	24.00	35.00
Saucer	4.50	8.50	9.50
Sugar, ftd	15.00	16.00	20.00
Tumbler, 9 oz, 4-1/4" h	35.00	38.00	50.00
Vegetable bowl, 10" l, oval	17.50	40.00	45.00

Above: Rosemary, amber vegetable bowl, **$17.50**; berry bowl, **$7.**

Right: Rosemary, green platter, **$24.**

Roulette

Many Windows

Manufactured by Hocking Glass Company, Lancaster, Ohio, from 1935 to 1939.

Made in crystal, green, and pink.

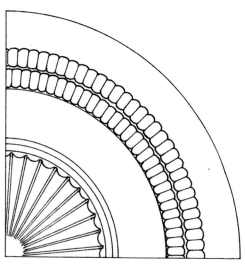

Item	Crystal	Green	Pink
Cup	35.00	8.50	8.50
Fruit bowl, 9" d	12.00	25.00	25.00
Iced tea tumbler, 12 oz, 5-1/8" h	24.00	40.00	35.00
Juice tumbler, 5 oz, 3-1/4" h	10.00	60.00	24.00
Old fashioned tumbler, 7-1/2 oz, 3-1/4" h	24.00	40.00	40.00
Pitcher, 65 oz, 8" h	30.00	35.00	45.00
Plate, 6" d, sherbet	3.50	4.50	5.00
Plate, 8-1/2" d, luncheon	7.00	8.00	6.00
Sandwich Plate, 12" d	15.00	18.50	20.00
Saucer	2.50	4.50	3.00
Sherbet	8.00	6.75	12.00
Tumbler, 9 oz, 4-1/8" h	15.00	20.00	30.00
Tumbler, 10 oz, 5-1/2" h, ftd	18.00	30.00	35.00
Whiskey, 1-1/2 oz, 2-1/2" h	10.00	18.00	17.50

Roulette, green plate, **$8**; sherbet, **$6.75**.

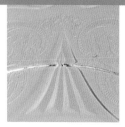

Royal Lace

Manufactured by Hazel Atlas Glass Company, Clarksburg, W.V. and Zanesville, Ohio, from 1934 to 1941.

Pieces are made in cobalt (Ritz) blue, crystal, green, pink, and some amethyst.

Reproductions: † Reproductions include a 5-ounce, 3-1/2-inch high tumbler, found in a darker cobalt blue. A cookie jar has also been reproduced in cobalt blue.

Item	Cobalt Blue	Crystal	Green	Pink
Berry bowl, 5" d	50.00	18.00	65.00	90.00
Berry bowl, 10" d	90.00	20.00	35.00	60.00
Bowl, 10" d, three legs, rolled edge	650.00	225.00	125.00	200.00
Bowl, 10" d, three legs, ruffled edge	750.00	95.00	125.00	165.00
Bowl, 10" d, three legs, straight edge	—	24.00	75.00	65.00
Butter dish, cov	865.00	90.00	275.00	200.00
Candlesticks, pr, rolled edge	—	45.00	85.00	280.00
Candlesticks, pr, ruffled edge	—	28.00	70.00	60.00
Candlesticks, pr, straight edge	—	35.00	75.00	55.00
Cookie jar, cov †	400.00	30.00	75.00	100.00
Cream soup, 4-3/4" d	50.00	18.00	35.00	30.00
Creamer, ftd	65.00	15.00	25.00	20.00
Cup and saucer	60.00	16.00	35.00	32.00
Nut bowl	1,500.00	275.00	425.00	425.00
Pitcher, 48 oz, straight sides	225.00	45.00	110.00	85.00
Pitcher, 64 oz, 8" h	295.00	45.00	120.00	125.00
Pitcher, 68 oz, 8" h, ice lip	320.00	60.00	—	115.00
Pitcher, 86 oz, 8" h	—	60.00	135.00	135.00
Pitcher, 96 oz, 9-1/2" h, ice lip	495.00	115.00	160.00	155.00
Plate, 6" d, sherbet	20.00	8.50	15.00	18.00
Plate, 8-1/2" d, luncheon	60.00	12.00	18.00	24.00
Plate, 9-7/8" d, dinner	55.00	25.00	45.00	40.00
Plate, 9-7/8" d, grill	40.00	20.00	25.00	22.50
Platter, 13" l, oval	60.00	30.00	45.00	48.00
Salt and pepper shakers, pr	395.00	65.00	130.00	85.00
Sherbet, ftd	50.00	18.00	60.00	35.00
Sherbet, metal holder	45.00	18.00	—	—
Sugar, cov	275.00	90.00	40.00	50.00
Sugar, open	—	15.00	25.00	20.00
Toddy or cider set	295.00	—	—	—
Tumbler, 5 oz, 3-1/2" h †	65.00	15.00	60.00	35.00
Tumbler, 9 oz, 4-1/8" h †	60.00	18.00	35.00	30.00
Tumbler, 10 oz, 4-7/8" h	245.00	25.00	60.00	60.00
Tumbler, 12 oz, 5-3/8" h	165.00	25.00	50.00	55.00
Vegetable bowl, 11" l, oval	60.00	25.00	35.00	95.00

Royal Lace, crystal dinner plate, **$25.**

Royal Ruby

Manufactured by Anchor Hocking Glass Corporation, Lancaster, Pa., from 1938 to 1967.

Pieces are made only in Royal Ruby.

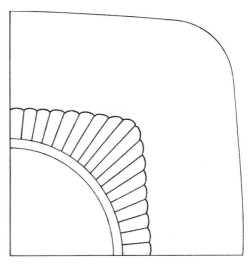

Item	Royal Ruby
Apothecary jar, 8-1/2" h	22.00
Ashtray, 3-1/2", sq	10.00
Ashtray, 4" d, round	10.00
Ashtray, 4-1/4", sq	10.00
Ashtray, 4-1/2", leaf	5.00
Ashtray, 5-7/8", sq	7.50
Ashtray, 7-3/4"	32.00
Beer bottle, 7 oz	42.50
Beer bottle, 12 oz	32.00
Beer bottle, 16 oz	35.00
Beer bottle, 32 oz	40.00
Berry bowl, 4-1/2" d, round	12.00
Berry bowl, 4-5/8" d, small, square	9.50
Berry bowl, 8-1/2" d, round	25.00
Bonbon, 6-1/2" d	20.00
Bowl, 7-3/8" w, sq	18.50
Bowl, 8-1/4" d, round	25.00
Bowl, 11" d, Rachael	50.00
Bowl, 12" l, oval, Rachael	70.00
Cereal bowl, 5-1/4" d	12.00
Cigarette box, card holder, 6-1/8" x 4"	90.00
Cocktail, 3-1/2 oz, Boopie	8.50
Cocktail, 3-1/2 oz, tumbler	10.00
Cordial, ftd	15.00
Creamer, flat	8.00
Creamer, ftd	10.00
Cup, round	12.00
Cup, square	7.50
Dessert bowl, 4-3/4" w, sq	12.00
Fruit bowl, 4-1/4" d	10.00
Goblet, 9 oz	9.00
Goblet, 9-1/2 oz	14.00
Goblet, ball stem	15.00
Ice bucket	55.00
Iced tea goblet, 14 oz, Boopie	20.00
Iced tea tumbler, 13 oz, 6" h, ftd	14.00
Ivy ball, 4" h, Wilson	10.00
Juice tumbler, 4 oz	7.00
Juice tumbler, 5-1/2 oz	10.00
Juice tumbler, 5 oz, flat or ftd	8.00
Juice pitcher, tilt, ball	40.00
Lamp	35.00
Marmalade, ruby top, crystal base	22.00

Item	Royal Ruby
Pitcher, 3 qt, tilted	45.00
Pitcher, 3 qt, upright	38.00
Pitcher, 42 oz, tilted	35.00
Pitcher, 42 oz, upright	40.00
Pitcher, 86 oz, 8-1/2"	35.00
Plate, 6-1/4" d, sherbet	6.50
Plate, 7" d, salad	5.50
Plate, 7-3/4" w, sq, salad	12.50
Plate, 8-3/8" w, sq, luncheon	12.00
Plate, 9-1/8" d, dinner	17.50
Plate, 13-3/4" d	35.00
Popcorn bowl, 5-1/4" d	12.50
Popcorn bowl, 10" d, deep	40.00
Puff box, ruby top, crystal base, orig label	28.00
Punch bowl and Stand	75.00
Punch set, 14 pieces	95.00
Punch cup	3.00
Relish, 3-3/4" x 8-3/4", tab handle	16.00
Roly poly tumbler	6.00
Salad bowl, 8-1/2" d	19.00
Salad bowl, 11-1/2" d	48.00
Saucer, 5-3/8" w, sq	4.00
Saucer, round	4.00
Set, 50 pcs, orig labels, orig box	350.00
Sherbet, Baltic, low collar	8.00
Sherbet, 6-1/2 oz, stemmed	9.50
Sherbet, 6 oz, Boopie	9.00
Shot glass	4.50
Soup bowl, 7-1/2" d	13.00
Sugar, flat	8.00
Sugar, footed	8.00
Sugar lid, notched	11.00
Tray, center handle, ruffled	16.50
Tumbler, 5 oz, 3-1/2" h	15.00
Tumbler, 9 oz, Windsor	8.00
Tumbler, 10 oz, 4-1/2" h, Baltic	10.00
Tumbler, 10 oz, 5" h, ftd	15.00
Tumbler, 12 oz, 4-7/8" h, ftd	16.00
Tumbler, 14 oz, 5" h	9.00
Tumbler, 15 oz, long boy	15.00
Tumbler, 16 oz, coupe	12.00
Vase, 3-3/4" h, Roosevelt	7.50
Vase, 4" h, Wilson, fancy edge	8.00
Vase, 6-3/8" h, Harding	9.00

Item	Royal Ruby	Item	Royal Ruby
Vase, 6-5/8" h, Coolidge	20.00	Vase, 10" h, fluted, star base	35.00
Vase, 9" h, Hoover, plain	20.00	Vase, 10" h, ftd, Rachael	50.00
Vase, 9" h, Hoover, white birds on branch dec	25.00	Vegetable bowl, 8" l, oval	30.00
		Wine, 2-1/2 oz, ftd	12.50

Royal Ruby, vase with original foil label, **$20.**

Royal Ruby, footed sugar, **$8**; footed creamer (on pedestal), **$10**; square cup, **$7.50**; square saucer, **$4**.

Royal Ruby, punch set, includes 14 pieces, punch bowl and six cups are shown, value for the entire set is **$95.**

Sandwich
Hocking

Manufactured by Hocking Glass Company, and later Anchor Hocking Corporation, from 1939 to 1964.

Pieces are made in crystal, Desert Gold, 1961-64; Forest Green, 1956-1960s; pink, 1939-1940; Royal Ruby, 1938-1939; and white/ivory (opaque), 1957-1960s.

Reproductions: † The cookie jar has been reproduced in crystal.

Item	Crystal	Desert Gold	Forest Green	Pink	Royal Ruby	White
Bowl, 4-5/16" d, smooth	5.00	—	4.00	—	—	—
Bowl, 4-7/8" d, smooth	5.00	6.00	—	7.00	17.50	—
Bowl, 4-7/8" d, crimped	20.00	—	—	—	—	—
Bowl, 5-1/4" d, scalloped	8.00	6.00	—	—	32.00	—
Bowl, 5-1/4" d, smooth	—	—	—	7.00	35.00	—
Bowl, 6-1/2" d, scalloped	7.50	9.00	60.00	—	35.00	—
Bowl, 6-1/2" d, smooth	7.50	6.00	—	—	—	—
Bowl, 7-1/4" d, scalloped	14.00	—	—	—	—	—
Bowl, 8-1/4" d, oval	6.00	—	—	—	—	—
Bowl, 8-1/4" d, scalloped	18.00	—	80.00	20.00	35.00	—
Butter dish, cov	45.00	—	—	—	—	—
Cereal bowl, 6-3/4" d	32.00	12.00	—	—	—	—
Cookie jar, cov † *	40.00	45.00	20.00	—	—	—
Creamer	7.50	—	30.00	—	—	—
Cup, coffee	3.50	12.00	24.00	—	—	—
Cup, tea	3.50	14.00	24.00	—	—	—
Custard cup	7.00	—	4.00	—	—	—
Custard cup liner	5.50	—	1.50	—	—	—
Custard cup, crimped	15.00	—	—	—	—	—
Dessert bowl, 5" d, crimped	18.50	—	—	—	—	—
Juice pitcher, 6" h	115.00	—	145.00	—	—	—
Juice tumbler, 3 oz, 3-3/8" h	12.00	—	6.00	—	—	—
Juice tumbler, 5 oz, 3-9/16" h	6.50	—	4.50	—	—	—
Pitcher, half gallon, ice lip	85.00	—	550.00	—	—	—
Plate, 6" d	5.00	—	—	—	—	—
Plate, 7" d, dessert	20.00	—	—	—	—	—
Plate, 8" d, luncheon	18.00	—	—	—	—	—
Plate, 9" d, dinner	24.00	9.00	125.00	10.00	—	—
Plate, 9" d, indent for punch cup	12.00	—	—	—	—	—
Punch bowl, 9-3/4" d	18.00	—	—	—	—	15.00
Punch bowl and stand	30.00	—	—	—	—	30.00
Punch bowl set, bowl, base, 12 cups	80.00	—	—	—	—	—
Punch cup	4.00	—	—	—	—	2.00
Salad bowl, 7" d	8.00	25.00	—	—	—	—
Salad bowl, 7-5/8" d	—	—	60.00	—	—	—
Salad bowl, 9" d	24.00	20.00	—	—	—	—
Sandwich plate, 12" d	14.00	17.50	—	—	—	—
Saucer	3.75	5.00	15.00	—	—	—
Sherbet, ftd	9.00	8.00	—	—	—	—
Snack set, plate and cup	12.50	—	—	—	—	—
Sugar, cov	30.00	—	—	—	—	—
Sugar, no cover	6.00	—	30.00	—	—	—
Tumbler, 9 oz, ftd	32.50	125.00	—	—	—	—
Tumbler, 9 oz, water	8.00	—	7.00	—	—	—
Vase	—	—	27.50	—	—	—
Vegetable, 8-1/2" l, oval	10.00	—	—	—	—	—

*No cover is known for the cookie jar in Forest Green.

Sandwich, Hocking, Forest Green cookie jar, no lid, **$10.**

Sandwich, Hocking, crystal oval bowl, **$6.**

Sandwich, Hocking, smooth Desert Gold bowl, 6-1/2" d, **$6.**

Sandwich, Hocking, crystal saucer, **$3.75.**

Sharon

Cabbage Rose

Manufactured by Federal Glass Company, Columbus, Ohio, from 1935 to 1939.

Pieces are made in amber, crystal, green, and pink.

Reproductions: † Reproductions include the butter dish, covered candy dish, creamer, covered sugar, and salt and pepper shakers. Reproduction colors include dark amber, blue, green, and pink.

Item	Amber	Crystal	Green	Pink
Berry bowl, 5" d	8.50	5.00	18.50	16.50
Berry bowl, 8-1/2" d	7.50	12.00	40.00	35.00
Butter dish, cov †	50.00	20.00	85.00	65.00
Cake plate, 11-1/2" d, ftd	30.00	10.00	65.00	45.00
Candy dish, cov †	45.00	15.00	100.00	65.00
Cereal bowl, 6" d	24.00	12.00	32.00	30.00
Champagne, 5" d bowl	—	—	—	12.00
Cheese dish, cov †	225.00	1,500.00	—	950.00
Cream soup, 5" d	28.00	15.00	60.00	52.50
Creamer, ftd †	15.00	14.00	22.00	20.00
Cup	9.00	6.00	18.00	18.00
Fruit bowl, 10-1/2" d	24.00	18.00	40.00	50.00
Iced tea tumbler, ftd	85.00	15.00	—	65.00
Jam dish, 7-1/2" d	45.00	—	48.00	215.00
Pitcher, 80 oz, ice lip	165.00	—	150.00	165.00
Pitcher, 80 oz, without ice lip	140.00	—	150.00	150.00
Plate, 6" d, bread and butter	12.00	5.00	9.00	9.50
Plate, 7-1/2" d, salad	22.50	6.50	8.00	30.00
Plate, 9-1/2" d, dinner	17.00	9.50	27.50	26.50
Platter, 12-1/2" l, oval	24.00	—	35.00	35.00
Salt and pepper shakers, pr †	50.00	—	80.00	65.00
Saucer	6.50	4.00	36.00	12.00
Sherbet, ftd	12.50	8.00	35.00	20.00
Soup, flat, 7-3/4" d, 1 7/8" deep	55.00	—	—	60.00
Sugar, cov †	35.00	12.00	55.00	60.00
Tumbler, 9 oz, 4-1/8" h, thick	30.00	—	65.00	47.50
Tumbler, 9 oz, 4-1/8" h, thin	38.00	—	65.00	50.00
Tumbler, 12 oz, 5-1/4" h, thick	55.00	—	95.00	50.00
Tumbler, 12 oz, 5-1/4" h, thin	55.00	—	95.00	62.00
Tumbler, 15 oz, 6-1/2" h, thick	125.00	18.00	—	65.00
Vegetable bowl, 9-1/2" l, oval	22.00	—	45.00	36.00

Sharon, pink sherbet, **$20**; berry bowl, 8-1/2 d, **$35**; creamer, **$20;** berry bowl, 5 d, **$16.50.**

REPRODUCTION!
Sharon, pink covered candy dish.

Ships

Sailboat, Sportsman Series

Manufactured by Hazel Atlas Glass Company, Clarksburg, W.V. and Zanesville, Ohio, late 1930s.

Pieces are made in cobalt blue with white, yellow, and red decoration. Pieces with yellow or red decoration are valued slightly higher than the traditional white decoration.

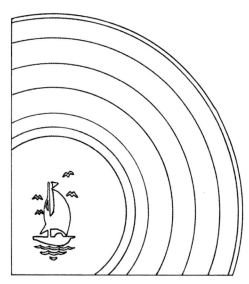

Item	Cobalt Blue with White Decoration	Item	Cobalt Blue with White Decoration
Ashtray	60.00	Pitcher, 86 oz, ice lip	75.00
Ashtray, metal sailboat	120.00	Plate, 5-7/8" d, bread and butter	40.00
Box, cov, three parts	250.00	Plate, 8" d, salad	27.50
Cocktail mixer, stirrer	45.00	Plate, 9" d, dinner	32.00
Cocktail shaker	25.00	Roly Poly, 6 oz	10.00
Cup	15.00	Saucer	18.00
Ice bowl	45.00	Shot glass, 2 oz, 2-1/4" h	250.00
Iced tea tumbler, 10-1/2 oz, 4-7/8" h	22.00	Tumbler, 4 oz, 3-1/4" h, heavy bottom	27.50
Iced tea tumbler, 12 oz	24.00	Tumbler, 4 oz, heavy bottom	12.00
Juice tumbler, 5 oz, 3-3/4" h	12.50	Tumbler, 9 oz, 3-3/4" h	18.00
Old fashioned tumbler, 8 oz, 3-3/8" h	22.00	Tumbler, 9 oz, 4-5/8" h	18.00
Pitcher, 82 oz, no ice lip	85.00	Whiskey, 3-1/2" h	45.00

Ships, cobalt blue cocktail shaker, **$25.**

Ships, cobalt blue salad plate, **$27.50.**

Sierra
Pinwheel

Manufactured by Jeannette Glass Company, Jeannette, Pa., from 1931 to 1933.

Pieces are made in green and pink. A few forms are known in Ultramarine.

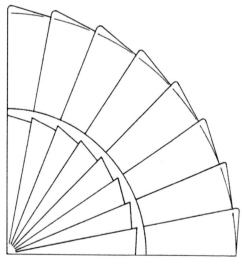

Item	Green	Pink
Berry, small	25.00	25.00
Berry bowl, 8-1/2" d	40.00	47.50
Butter dish, cov	80.00	85.00
Cereal bowl, 5-1/2" d	35.00	30.00
Creamer	25.00	25.00
Cup	18.50	15.00
Pitcher, 32 oz, 6-1/2" h	170.00	150.00
Plate, 9" d, dinner	30.00	30.00
Platter, 11" l, oval	70.00	55.00
Salt and pepper shakers, pr	50.00	50.00
Saucer	12.00	8.00
Serving tray, 10-1/4" l, two handles	25.00	28.00
Sugar, cov	48.00	48.00
Tumbler, 9 oz, 4-1/2" h, ftd	90.00	80.00
Vegetable bowl, 9-1/4" l, oval	185.00	95.00

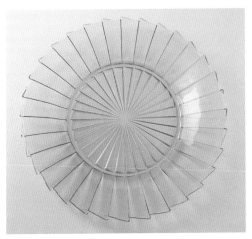

Sierra, green butter dish, **$80**; and pink cup, **$15**; and saucer, **$8**.

Sierra, pink dinner plate, **$30**.

Sunburst
Herringbone

Manufactured by Jeannette Glass Company, Jeannette, Pa., late 1930s.

Pieces are made in crystal.

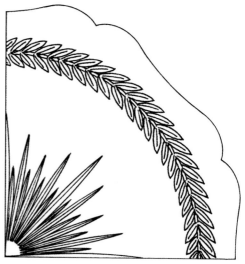

Item	Crystal	Item	Crystal
Berry bowl, 4-3/4" d	9.00	Plate, 9-1/4" d, dinner	25.00
Berry bowl, 8-1/2" d	18.00	Relish, two parts	14.50
Bowl, 10-1/2" d	25.00	Salad bowl, 11" d	30.00
Candlesticks, pr, double	35.00	Sandwich plate, 11-3/4" d	15.00
Creamer, ftd	16.00	Saucer	4.00
Cup	7.50	Sherbet	12.00
Cup and saucer	10.00	Sugar	16.00
Plate, 5-1/2" d	12.00	Tumbler, 4" h, 9 oz, flat	18.50

Sunburst, crystal sandwich plate, **$15.**

Sunflower

Manufactured by Jeannette Glass Company, Jeannette, Pa., 1930s.

Pieces are made in Delphite, green, pink, and some opaque colors. Look for a creamer in Delphite that is valued at $85.

Item	Delphite	Green	Pink	Opaque
Ashtray, 5" d	—	15.00	15.00	—
Cake plate, 10" d, three legs	—	20.00	30.00	—
Creamer	90.00	20.00	20.00	85.00
Cup	—	15.00	18.00	75.00
Plate, 9" d, dinner	—	27.50	24.00	—
Saucer	—	13.50	12.00	85.00
Sugar	—	25.00	22.00	—
Trivet, 7" d, three legs, turned up edge	—	325.00	315.00	—
Tumbler, 8 oz, 4-3/8" h, ftd	—	35.00	32.00	—

Sunflower, green cake plate, **$20.**

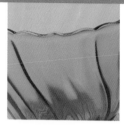

Swirl

Petal Swirl

Manufactured by Jeannette Glass Company, Jeannette, Pa., from 1937 to 1938.

Pieces are made in amber, Delphite, ice blue, pink and Ultramarine. Production was limited in amber and ice blue.

Swirl, Ultramarine sugar, **$18**; creamer, **$18**.

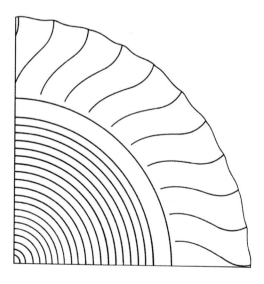

Item	Delphite	Pink	Ultramarine
Berry bowl	15.00	—	18.50
Bowl, 10" d, ftd, closed handles	—	25.00	35.00
Butter dish, cov	—	220.00	245.00
Candleholders, pr, double branch	—	40.00	60.00
Candleholders, pr, single branch	115.00	—	—
Candy dish, cov	—	235.00	150.00
Candy dish, open, three legs	—	20.00	20.00
Cereal bowl, 5-1/4" d	15.00	15.00	16.00
Coaster, 1" x 3-1/4"	—	18.00	18.00
Console bowl, 10-1/2" d, ftd	—	20.00	35.00
Creamer	12.00	9.50	18.00
Cup and saucer	17.50	16.00	20.00
Plate, 6-1/2" d, sherbet	6.50	8.00	9.00
Plate, 7-1/4" d, luncheon	—	6.50	15.00
Plate, 8" d, salad	9.00	8.50	18.00
Plate, 9-1/4" d, dinner	12.00	17.50	25.00
Plate, 10-1/2" d, dinner	18.00	—	30.00
Platter, 12" l, oval	35.00	—	—
Salad bowl, 9" d	30.00	18.00	32.50
Salad bowl, 9" d, rimmed	—	20.00	30.00
Salt and pepper shakers, pr	—	—	55.00
Sandwich plate, 12-1/2" d	—	20.00	32.50
Sherbet, low, ftd	—	24.00	28.00
Soup, tab handles, lug	—	25.00	52.50
Sugar, ftd	—	12.00	18.00
Tray, 10-1/2" l, two handles	25.00	—	—
Tumbler, 9 oz, 4" h	—	18.00	35.00
Tumbler, 9 oz, 4-5/8" h	—	18.00	—
Tumbler, 13 oz, 5-1/8" h	—	45.00	90.00
Vase, 6-1/2" h, ftd, ruffled	—	22.00	—
Vase, 8-1/2" h, ftd or flat	—	—	30.00

Swirl, Ultramarine dinner plate, 10-1/2" d, **$30**; bowl with closed handles, **$35.**

Tea Room

Manufactured by Indiana Glass Company, Dunkirk, Ind., from 1926 to 1931.

Pieces are made in amber, crystal, green and pink.

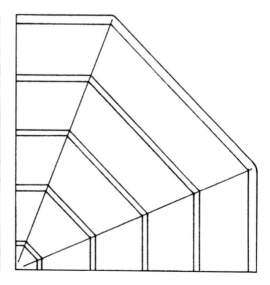

Item	Amber	Crystal	Green	Pink
Banana split bowl, 7-1/2" l	—	95.00	200.00	215.00
Candlesticks, pr, low	—	—	80.00	95.00
Celery bowl, 8-1/2" d	—	15.00	35.00	27.50
Creamer, 3-1/4" h	—	—	30.00	28.00
Creamer, 4-1/2" h, ftd	80.00	—	20.00	25.00
Creamer and sugar on tray	—	—	95.00	85.00
Cup	—	—	65.00	60.00
Finger bowl	—	80.00	50.00	40.00
Goblet, 9 oz	—	—	75.00	65.00
Ice bucket	—	—	85.00	80.00
Lamp, electric	—	140.00	175.00	195.00
Mustard, cov	—	145.00	160.00	140.00
Parfait	—	—	72.00	65.00
Pitcher, 64 oz	425.00	400.00	150.00	200.00
Plate, 6-1/2" d, sherbet	—	—	35.00	32.00
Plate, 8-1/4" d, luncheon	—	—	37.50	35.00
Plate, 10-1/2" d, two handles	—	—	50.00	45.00
Relish, divided	—	—	30.00	25.00
Salad bowl, 8-3/4" d, deep	—	—	150.00	135.00
Salt and pepper shakers, pr, ftd	—	—	60.00	55.00
Saucer	—	—	30.00	25.00
Sherbet	—	22.00	40.00	35.00
Sugar, 3" h, cov	—	—	115.00	100.00
Sugar, 4-1/2" h, ftd	80.00	—	30.00	30.00
Sugar, cov, flat	—	—	200.00	170.00
Sundae, ftd, ruffled	—	—	85.00	70.00
Tumbler, 6 oz, ftd	—	—	55.00	32.00
Tumbler, 8 oz, 5-1/4" h, ftd	75.00	—	32.00	40.00
Tumbler, 11 oz, ftd	—	—	45.00	45.00
Tumbler, 12 oz, ftd	—	—	60.00	55.00
Vase, 6-1/2" h, ruffled edge	—	—	145.00	90.00
Vase, 9-1/2" h, ruffled	—	45.00	175.00	100.00
Vase, 9-1/2" h, straight	—	130.00	95.00	225.00
Vase, 11" h, ruffled edge	—	—	350.00	395.00
Vase, 11" h, straight	—	—	200.00	395.00
Vegetable bowl, 9-1/2" l, oval	—	—	75.00	65.00

Tea Room, pink footed sugar, **$30.**

Tea Room, pink footed creamer, **$35.**

Thistle

Manufactured by Macbeth-Evans, Charleroi, Pa., from about 1929 to 1930.

Pieces are made in crystal, green, pink, and yellow. Production was limited in crystal and yellow pieces.

Reproductions: † Recent reproductions have been found in pink, a darker emerald green, and wisteria. Several of the reproductions have a scalloped edge. Reproductions include the cake plate, fruit bowl, pitcher, salt and pepper shakers, and a small tumbler.

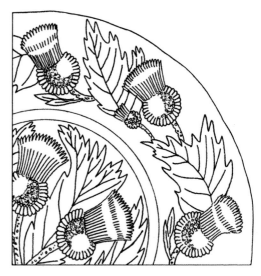

Item	Green	Pink
Cake plate, 13" d, heavy †	195.00	225.00
Cereal bowl, 5-1/2" d	50.00	50.00
Cup, thin	36.50	24.00
Fruit bowl, 10-1/4" d †	295.00	495.00
Plate, 8" d, luncheon	30.00	32.00
Plate, 10-1/4" d, grill	35.00	30.00
Saucer	12.00	12.00

Thistle, green luncheon plate, **$30.**

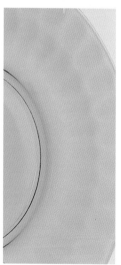

Thumbprint

Manufactured by Federal Glass Company, Columbus, Ohio, from 1927 to 1930.

Pieces are made in green.

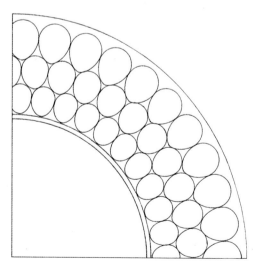

Item	Green	Item	Green
Berry bowl, 4-3/4" d	10.00	Plate, 9-1/4" d, dinner	24.00
Berry bowl, 8" d	25.00	Salt and pepper shakers, pr	65.00
Cereal bowl, 5" d	10.00	Saucer	4.00
Creamer, ftd	12.00	Sherbet	9.00
Cup	8.00	Sugar, ftd	12.00
Fruit bowl, 5" d	10.00	Tumbler, 5" h	25.00
Juice tumbler, 4" h	6.00	Tumbler, 5-1/2" h	10.00
Plate, 6" d, sherbet	4.50	Whiskey, 1-7/8" h	18.00
Plate, 8" d, luncheon	7.00	Whiskey, 2-1/4" h	6.50

Thumbprint, green luncheon plate, **$7.**

Twisted Optic

Manufactured by Imperial Glass Company, Bellaire, Ohio, from 1927 to 1930.

Pieces are made in amber, blue, canary, green, and pink.

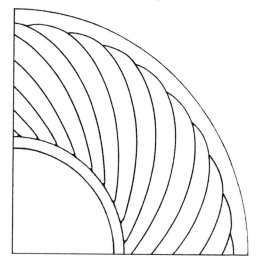

Twisted Optic, pink sherbet plate, 6" d, **$3.**

Item	Amber	Blue	Canary	Green	Pink
Basket, 10" h	55.00	95.00	95.00	60.00	60.00
Bowl, 7" d, ruffled	—	—	—	—	18.00
Bowl, 9" d	18.50	28.50	28.50	18.50	18.50
Bowl, 11-1/2" d, 4-1/4" h	24.00	48.00	48.00	24.00	24.00
Candlesticks, pr, 3" h	22.00	40.00	40.00	35.00	22.00
Candlesticks, pr, 8" h	30.00	50.00	50.00	30.00	30.00
Candy jar, cov, flat	25.00	50.00	50.00	25.00	25.00
Candy jar, cov, flat, flange edge	50.00	90.00	90.00	55.00	55.00
Candy jar, cov, ftd, flange edge	50.00	90.00	90.00	55.00	55.00
Candy jar, cov, ftd, short	55.00	100.00	100.00	60.00	60.00
Candy jar, cov, ftd, tall	55.00	100.00	100.00	60.00	60.00
Cereal bowl, 5" d	8.50	15.00	15.00	10.00	10.00
Cologne bottle, stopper	60.00	85.00	85.00	60.00	60.00
Console bowl, 10-1/2" d	25.00	45.00	45.00	25.00	25.00
Cream soup, 4-3/4" d	12.00	25.00	25.00	15.00	15.00
Creamer	8.00	14.00	14.00	8.00	8.00
Cup	7.50	12.50	12.50	5.00	8.00
Mayonnaise	20.00	50.00	50.00	30.00	30.00
Pitcher, 64 oz	45.00	—	—	40.00	45.00
Plate, 6" d, sherbet	3.00	6.50	6.50	3.00	3.00
Plate, 7" d, salad	4.00	8.00	8.00	4.00	4.00
Plate, 7-1/2" x 9" l, oval	6.00	12.00	12.00	6.00	6.00
Plate, 8" d, luncheon	6.00	9.00	10.00	6.00	5.00
Powder jar, cov	38.00	65.00	65.00	38.00	38.00
Preserve jar	30.00	—	—	30.00	30.00
Salad bowl, 7" d	12.00	25.00	25.00	15.00	15.00
Sandwich plate, 10" d	12.00	20.00	20.00	15.00	15.00
Sandwich server, center handle	22.00	35.00	35.00	22.00	22.00
Sandwich server, two-handles, flat	15.00	20.00	20.00	15.00	15.00
Saucer	2.50	4.50	4.50	2.50	5.00
Sherbet	7.50	12.00	12.50	7.00	7.50
Sugar	8.00	14.00	14.00	8.00	10.00
Tumbler, 4-1/2" h, 9 oz	6.50	—	—	6.50	7.00
Tumbler, 5-1/4" h, 12 oz	9.50	—	—	9.50	10.00
Vase, 7-1/4" h, two handles, rolled edge	35.00	65.00	65.00	40.00	40.00
Vase, 8" h, two handles, fan	45.00	95.00	95.00	50.00	50.00
Vase, 8" h, two handles, straight edge	45.00	95.00	95.00	50.00	50.00

U.S. Swirl

Manufactured by U.S. Glass Company, late 1920s.

Pieces are made in crystal, green, iridescent, and pink. Production in crystal and iridescent was limited.

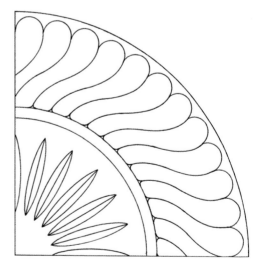

Item	Green	Pink
Berry bowl, 4-3/8" d	8.00	10.00
Berry bowl, 7-7/8" d	15.00	17.00
Bowl, 5-1/2" d, handle	10.00	12.00
Bowl, 8-1/4" l, 2 3/4" h, oval	40.00	40.00
Bowl, 8-3/8" l, 1-3/4" h, oval	50.00	50.00
Butter dish, cov	115.00	115.00
Candy, cov, two handles	30.00	32.00
Creamer	15.00	17.50
Pitcher, 48 oz, 8" h	55.00	50.00
Plate, 6-1/8" d, sherbet	3.00	2.50
Plate, 7-7/8" d, salad	6.00	6.50
Salt and pepper shakers, pr	48.00	45.00
Sherbet, 3-1/4" h	5.00	6.00
Sugar, cov	35.00	32.00
Tumbler, 8 oz, 3-5/8" h	12.00	12.00
Tumbler, 12 oz, 4-3/4" h	15.00	17.50
Vase, 6-1/2" h	25.00	25.00

U.S. Swirl, green pitcher, **$55.**

Vernon
No. 616

Manufactured by Indiana Glass Company, Dunkirk, Ind., from 1930 to 1932.

Pieces are made in crystal, green, and yellow.

Item	Crystal	Green	Yellow
Creamer, ftd	12.00	25.00	30.00
Cup	10.00	15.00	18.00
Plate, 8" d, luncheon	7.00	10.00	15.00
Sandwich plate, 11-1/2" d	14.00	25.00	30.00
Saucer	4.00	6.00	6.00
Sugar, ftd	18.00	25.00	30.00
Tumbler, 5" h, ftd	16.00	40.00	45.00

Vernon, yellow tumbler, **$45.**

Victory

Manufactured by Diamond Glass-Ware Company, Indiana, Pa., from 1929 to 1932.

Pieces are made in amber, black, cobalt blue, green, and pink.

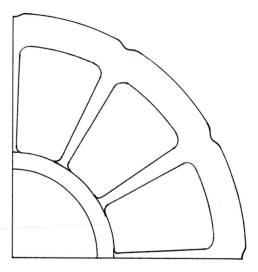

Item	Amber	Black	Cobalt Blue	Green	Pink
Bonbon, 7" d	15.00	20.00	20.00	15.00	15.00
Bowl, 11" d, rolled edge	30.00	50.00	50.00	30.00	30.00
Bowl, 12-1/2" d, flat edge	30.00	60.00	60.00	30.00	30.00
Candlesticks, pr, 3" h	35.00	100.00	100.00	35.00	35.00
Cereal bowl, 6-1/2" d	15.00	30.00	30.00	15.00	15.00
Cheese and cracker set,12" d indented plate and comport	45.00	—	—	45.00	45.00
Comport, 6" h, 6-1/4" d	18.00	—	—	18.00	18.00
Console bowl, 12" d	35.00	65.00	65.00	35.00	35.00
Creamer	17.50	45.00	45.00	15.00	15.00
Cup	10.00	35.00	40.00	10.00	10.00
Goblet, 7 oz, 5" h	20.00	—	—	20.00	20.00
Gravy boat, underplate	185.00	325.00	325.00	185.00	185.00
Mayonnaise set, 3-1/2" h, 5-1/2" d bowl, 8-1/2" d indented plate, ladle	55.00	100.00	100.00	55.00	55.00
Plate, 6" d, bread and butter	6.50	17.50	17.50	6.50	6.50
Plate, 7" d, salad	7.50	20.00	20.00	8.00	7.00
Plate, 8" d, luncheon	10.00	40.00	30.00	8.00	8.00
Plate, 9" d, dinner	20.00	40.00	40.00	22.00	20.00
Platter, 12" l, oval	30.00	70.00	70.00	32.00	32.00
Sandwich server, center handle	35.00	65.00	65.00	40.00	30.00
Saucer	5.00	12.50	12.50	5.00	6.00
Sherbet, ftd	15.00	27.50	27.50	15.00	15.00
Soup bowl, 8-1/2" d, flat	20.00	45.00	45.00	20.00	20.00
Sugar	15.00	45.00	45.00	15.00	15.00
Vegetable bowl, 9" l, oval	35.00	85.00	85.00	35.00	35.00

Victory, pink creamer, **$15**; sugar, **$15**.

Waterford
Waffle

Manufactured by Hocking Glass Company, Lancaster, Ohio, from 1938 to 1944.

Pieces are made in crystal, Forest Green (1950s), pink, white, and yellow. Forest Green production was limited; currently an ashtray is valued at $5. Yellow was also limited. Collector interest is low in white.

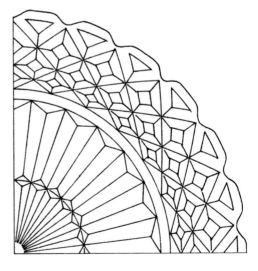

Item	Crystal	Pink
Ashtray, 4" d	8.00	—
Berry bowl, 4-3/4" d	8.50	18.00
Berry bowl, 8-1/4" d	10.00	36.00
Bonbon, cov	45.00	—
Butter dish, cov	30.00	250.00
Cake plate, 10-1/4" d, handles	15.00	25.00
Cereal bowl, 5-1/2" d	18.50	32.00
Coaster, 4" d	5.50	—
Creamer, Miss America style	35.00	—
Creamer, oval	5.00	15.00
Cup	8.50	18.00
Cup, Miss America style	—	45.00
Goblet, 5-1/4" h	16.00	—
Goblet, 5-1/2" h, Miss America style	35.00	85.00
Goblet, 5-5/8" h	20.00	—
Juice pitcher, 42 oz, tilted	30.00	—
Juice tumbler, 5 oz, 3-1/2" h, Miss America style	—	65.00
Lamp, 4" spherical base	45.00	—
Pitcher, 80 oz, tilted, ice lip	50.00	165.00
Plate, 6" d, sherbet	5.00	9.50
Plate, 7-1/8" d, salad	8.00	18.00
Plate, 9-5/8" d, dinner	12.00	24.00
Platter, 14" l	14.00	—
Relish, 13-3/4" d, five parts	12.00	—
Relish, 14" d, six parts	35.00	—
Salt and pepper shakers, pr	14.50	—
Sandwich plate, 13-3/4" d	15.00	32.00
Saucer	5.00	5.00
Sherbet, ftd	5.00	15.00
Sherbet, ftd, scalloped base	8.00	—
Sugar	6.50	15.00
Sugar, Miss America style	30.00	—
Sugar lid, oval	5.00	25.00
Tray, 10-1/4" l, handles	15.00	—
Tray, 13" d	15.00	45.00
Tumbler, 10 oz, 4-7/8" h, ftd	12.00	30.00

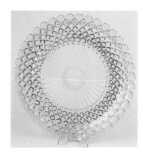

Waterford, crystal dinner plate, **$12.**

Windsor

Windsor Diamond

Manufactured by Jeannette Glass Company, Jeannette, Pa., from 1936 to 1946.

Pieces are made in crystal, green, and pink, with limited production in amberina red, Delphite, and ice blue.

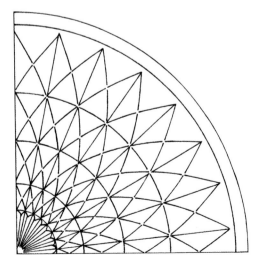

Item	Crystal	Green	Pink
Ashtray, 5-3/4" d	15.00	55.00	45.00
Berry bowl, 4-3/4" d	5.00	5.00	12.00
Berry bowl, 8-1/2" d	7.50	18.50	25.00
Bowl, 5" l, pointed edge	10.00	—	70.00
Bowl, 7" x 11-3/4", boat shape	30.00	40.00	32.00
Bowl, 7-1/2" d, three legs	8.00	—	24.00
Bowl, 8" d, two handles	9.00	24.00	20.00
Bowl, 8" l, pointed edge	10.00	—	48.00
Bowl, 10-1/2" l, pointed edge	25.00	—	32.00
Butter dish, cov	30.00	95.00	60.00
Cake plate, 10-3/4" d, ftd	12.00	22.00	20.00
Candlesticks, pr, 3" h	24.00	—	265.00
Candy jar, cov	18.00	—	—
Cereal bowl, 5-3/8" d	10.00	32.50	32.00
Chop plate, 13-5/8" d	24.00	55.00	45.00
Coaster, 3-1/4" d	8.50	22.00	25.00
Comport	9.00	—	—
Cream soup, 5" d	6.00	30.00	25.00
Creamer	8.00	15.00	20.00
Creamer, Holiday shape	7.50	—	—
Cup	7.00	18.00	12.00
Fruit console, 12-1/2" d	45.00	—	115.00
Iced tea tumbler, 12 oz, 5" h	—	55.00	—
Pitcher, 16 oz, 4-1/2" h	25.00	—	115.00
Pitcher, 52 oz, 6-3/4" h	20.00	65.00	40.00
Plate, 6" d, sherbet	3.75	8.00	6.00
Plate, 7" d, salad	4.50	30.00	18.00
Plate, 9" d, dinner	10.00	25.00	25.00
Platter, 11-1/2" l, oval	7.00	25.00	30.00
Powder jar	20.00	—	55.00
Relish platter, 11-1/2" l, divided	30.00	—	200.00
Salad bowl, 10-1/2" d	12.00	—	—
Salt and pepper shakers, pr	20.00	55.00	45.00
Sandwich plate, 10" d, closed handles	10.00	—	24.00
Sandwich plate, 10" d, open handles	12.50	18.00	20.00
Saucer	2.50	5.00	4.50
Sherbet, ftd	3.50	18.50	15.00
Sugar, cov	24.00	40.00	42.00
Sugar, cov, Holiday shape	12.00	—	135.00
Tray, 4" sq	5.00	12.00	10.00
Tray, 4" sq, handles	6.00	—	40.00
Tray, 4-1/8" x 9"	5.00	16.00	10.00
Tray, 4-1/8" x 9", handles	9.00	—	50.00

Item	Crystal	Green	Pink
Tray, 8-1/2" x 9-3/4"	7.00	35.00	25.00
Tray, 8-1/2" x 9-3/4", handles	15.00	45.00	85.00
Tumbler, 4" h, ftd	7.00	—	—
Tumbler, 5 oz, 3-1/4" h	9.00	36.50	26.50
Tumbler, 7-1/4" h, ftd	19.00	—	—
Tumbler, 9 oz, 4" h	7.50	36.50	18.00
Tumbler, 10 oz, 5-1/4" h, ftd	12.00	—	—
Tumbler, 11 oz, 4-5/8" h	8.00	—	—
Tumbler, 11 oz, 5" h, ftd	12.00	—	—
Tumbler, 12 oz, 5" h	11.00	55.00	32.50
Vegetable bowl, 9-1/2" l, oval	7.50	32.50	25.00

Windsor, crystal chop plate, **$24**; pink pitcher, 16 oz, **$115.**

Yorktown

Manufactured by Federal Glass Company in the mid-1950s.

Pieces are made in crystal, iridescent, smoke, white, and yellow. Values for all the colors are about the same.

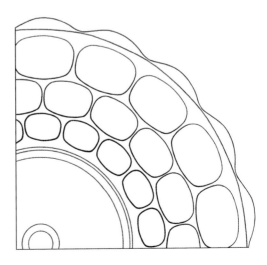

Item	Crystal
Berry bowl, 5-1/2" d	4.50
Berry bowl, 9-1/2" d	10.00
Celery tray, 10" l	10.00
Creamer	5.00
Cup	3.50
Fruit bowl, 10" d, ftd	18.00
Iced tea tumbler, 5-1/4" h, 13 oz	7.50
Juice tumbler, 3-7/8" h, 6 oz	4.50
Mug	15.00
Plate, 8-1/4" d	4.50
Plate, 11-1/2" d	8.50

Item	Crystal
Punch bowl set	40.00
Punch cup	2.50
Relish	3.00
Sandwich server	4.50
Saucer	1.00
Sherbet, 7 oz	3.50
Snack cup	2.50
Snack plate with indent	3.50
Sugar	5.00
Tumbler, 4-3/4" h, 10 oz	6.00
Vase, 8" h	15.00

Yorktown, crystal fruit bowl, **$18.**

Yorktown, yellow sandwich server with gold metal center handle, **$4.50.**

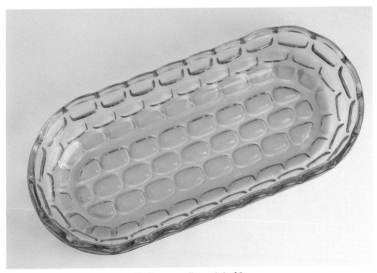

Yorktown, yellow relish, **$3.**

Glossary

AOP: All-over pattern; often found in descriptions to indicate a design that covers the entire piece rather than in just one location.

Berry Bowl: Used to describe both individual serving dishes and a master bowl used as a set to serve different kinds of berries. Often accompanied by a creamer or milk pitcher and sugar bowl.

Bouillon: Generally, a cup-shaped bowl for serving broth or clear soups; usually has handles.

Cheese and Cracker Set: Serving set often consists of a comport to hold cheese and large plate for crackers; forms differ. Sometimes a sherbet is used as a comport.

Cheese Dish: Serving dish, often with domed top, to cover a cheese wedge.

Children's Wares: Dish and tea sets designed to be used by children for play.

Chop Plate: Large round plate used to serve individual portions of meat and fowl.

Cider Set: Consists of covered cookie jar (used to hold cider), tray, and roly-poly cups and ladle.

Closed Handle: Solid glass handle.

Comport: Container used as a serving dish, open with handles, sometimes covered.

Compote: Another name for comport.

Console Set: Decorative large bowl with matching candlesticks.

Cream Soup: Bowl used to serve cream-type or chilled soups, usually has handles.

Cup and Saucer: Used to refer to place-setting cup and saucer; some patterns include larger coffee cup or more diminutive tea cup.

Demitasse Cup and Saucer: Term used to describe smaller cup and saucer used for after-dinner beverage.

Domino Tray: Tray used to hold sugar blocks shaped like dominoes.

Eggcup: Stemware with short stem used to hold an egg, usually used with an underplate.

Goblet: Stemware used to hold water.

Grill Plate: Dinner-sized plate with lines that divide the plate into compartments.

Ice Lip: Small piece of glass inside of top of pitcher to hold ice in the pitcher. May also mean a pinched lip that prevents ice from falling from a pitcher.

Icer: Vessel with compartment to hold crushed ice to keep main vessel cold, i.e., mayonnaise, cream soup, shrimp, etc.

Individual-Sized Pieces: Smaller-sized pieces, often designed for bed tray use. Not to be confused with children's wares.

Liner: Underplate or under bowl used to accompany another piece, i.e., finger bowl or sherbet.

Light (Lite): Branch found on candlestick used to hold additional candles, i.e., two light, three light.

Nappy: Shallow bowl used as serving dish or in a place setting; often has small handle.

Oil/Vinegar: Term used to describe a cruet or bottle with a stopper to hold oil and/or vinegar for salads.

Platter: Small, medium, or large oval plate used to serve roasts and fowl.

Ring Handle: Figural round handle, ring-shaped.

Salver: Large round plate used as serving piece.

Sandwich Server: Round plate, often with center handle (made of glass or metal) used to serve tea-type sandwiches.

Sherbet: Part of a place setting used to hold sherbet, often served with matching underplate about the same size as a saucer.

Snack Set: Plate or small tray with indent to hold punch or coffee-type cup.

Spooner: Small, often squatty, open vase-type vessel used to hold spoons upright. Typically, part of table set.

Spoon Tray: Small bowl-shaped vessel used to hold spoons horizontally, often oval. Often used on buffets, etc., to hold extra place-setting spoons.

Stand: Base or additional piece used to hold punch bowl, etc.

Table Set: Name given to set of matching covered butter dish, creamer, covered (or open) sugar, and spooner. An extended table service may include syrup, toothpick holder, and salt and pepper shakers.

Tab Handle: Small solid glass handle useful to grab bowl, etc.

Toddy Set: Set consists of covered cookie jar (used to hold toddy), tray, and roly-poly cups and ladle.

Tumbler: Any footed or flat vessel used to hold water or other liquids. Specialized tumblers include ginger ale, juice, iced tea, lemonade, old fashioned, and whiskey.

Wine: Term used to describe stemware that holds wine. Depression-era wines have a small capacity by today's standards.

Index

Patterns By Manufacturer